HOW TO LIVE
WITH YOUR
HUSBAND

Also by Mary Killen

Best Behaviour – The *Tatler* Book of
Alternative Etiquette

Dear Mary – The Spectator
Book of Solutions

HOW TO LIVE WITH YOUR HUSBAND

MARY KILLEN

HEINEMANN : LONDON

First published in Great Britain 1996
by William Heinemann
an imprint of Reed International Books Ltd
Michelin House, 81 Fulham Road, London SW3 6RB
and Auckland, Melbourne, Singapore and Toronto

A CIP catalogue record for this title
is available from the British Library

ISBN 0 434 00275 5

Typeset in 11.5 on 14 point Bembo
by Deltatype Ltd, Birkenhead, Merseyside
Printed and bound in Great Britain by
Clays Ltd, St Ives plc

To Joey, Sophy, Louise,
Ripples, Cressida and Frances,
who suffer so stoically,
and to my husband, Giles
without whom this book
would never have been possible.

Including . . .

BABIES – witnessing delivery of; BABYISHNESS – over food;
BARBECUES – jostling for role as dominant male; BEER –
and personality change; BRAVERY – compared to war heroes;
CHIPPINESS – with upper classes; CLUTTER – dislike of
and chucking out of wife's valued possessions; COOKING –
criticism of wife's; CRIME AND PUNISHMENT – domestic;
DECISIONS – so many to make; DIRECTIONS – inability to
follow; DIY – the real costs; DRIVING – fear when in car with
him; EARPLUGS – as an aid to marital harmony; EATING –
with mouth open and using repetitive smearing action to load
food on to fork; ECONOMIES – false; END OF EMPIRE –
resultant thwarting of his leadership skills; EYESORES – love
of pointing out when driving; FAWLTYISM – Basil; FIND
THINGS – inability to; HEATERS – turning off;
HITLERISM – Little; KEYS – persistent losing of; MISTAKES
– joy in catching wife out in making; MONEY – wasting;
MOTHERS-IN-LAW – his and yours; NANNY – how he
turns you into one; NEGORRHOEA – or perma-grumbling;
PACKING – Pyrrhic; POLICING – of wife and daily;
PROJECTION – of own vices; RIVALRY – with friends;
SECRETS – blabbing out at dinner parties; SHOPPING –
impatience with wife; STUPIDITY – generalised; THINK –
unwillingness to; TIN POT DICTATORISM; TRAFFIC
JAMS; WORKMEN – siding against wife with;
WORRYING – at things that are not yet broken so that they
break . . .

CONTENTS

INTRODUCTION

He's so annoying — but then, so are all his friends.

'How much did you spend on Charlotte's present?' enquired Giles one morning as I unpacked my basket on the kitchen table.

'Four ninety-nine for a tape of *Five Go Adventuring Again* by Enid Blyton,' I answered, my eyes popping in mock excitement as I waved the tape at our small daughter.

Freya shook her head woefully. 'She won't like that,' she said. 'Charlotte would rather have had stickers.'

Giles added to the annoyance. 'That's far too much,' he said. 'One, or at most two pounds, is about the right amount to spend on a present to bring to a child's birthday party.'

'You don't know what you're talking about,' I scowled. 'Five pounds is the correct amount, isn't it Melly?' I urged our nanny.

'Yes,' she nodded sagely. 'About five pounds is the average.'

'So stay out of women's business!' I raged, storming into my little office where I locked the door to prevent any of them from coming in.

The phone was ringing. 'Giles is so annoying,' I told his best friend Harry who was ringing on a crackly line from Kenya.

'I know Giles is annoying,' said Harry in steady defence. 'But think of this — imagine that you were married to any one of your best friends' husbands, and given that you were in love with them, would you find any one of them any less annoying?'

I thought through the roll call. Gerry, Mal, Cyril, Hugh . . . they were all wildly annoying in their own right! What if I had been married to Gerry who, when he and his wife were really broke, wrote out a cheque for two thousand pounds to join the Meridien Health Club in Piccadilly? Jo went bananas when she saw the bank statement. 'Look,' said Gerry. 'It's round the corner from my office. I can go there before work and I can go there after work. I'll want to go there because it's so luxurious it will be a treat rather than a punishment. You won't be able to keep me away from there. Now do you want me to be dead or do you want us to owe two thousand pounds?' How many times did Gerry go to the Meridien Health Club during the year of his membership? Once. The time he joined and wrote the cheque.

Then there is Hugh, a writer who, instead of learning to type himself, sends handwritten batches by expensive motorcycle messengers to a typist at the other end of London. He claims he cannot send the pages by fax because he likes the 'great satisfaction of handing over the document to a messenger and being able to feel the *physical* relief of getting rid of the burden'. On numerous occasions, having ordered a bike, he has found that lethargy or writer's block has prevented him from actually getting any writing ready for the typist. Ashamed to admit this to the motorcycle messenger he has handed him an envelope stuffed with blank pieces of paper.

Harry, I remembered, once used the sharp edge of his son's dummy to flick compacted cow-pat out of the zig-zagged rubber sole of his shoe. Then he handed the dummy back to the toddler to suck.

Some people depend on soap operas for a sense of continuity in their lives, others depend on day-to-day updates on their friends' minor domestic disputes. They target marital relationships they can identify with in the hope of salvaging some succour from shared ordeals and annoyances.

Susie's husband, like mine, secretly longs for a job in the police force, and lives for catching her out in some petty crime. 'He is always catching me,' she says, 'doing things like using the telephone in the car because he's on the one in the house. Then I forget to turn the ignition off so the batteries are dead in the morning. It makes him so happy.'

My mother was surprised to see me fuming a year after my marriage as Giles banged in and out of the house looking for his car keys, turning the contents of drawers out all over the floor and shouting 'Who's hidden them?'. As we sat in the car waiting my mother stared ahead in calm acceptance of the delay. 'Why are you getting cross?' she asked serenely. 'Do you not know that all men are annoying?'

She was right, as I was to find out when I began to write about Giles in the *Sunday Telegraph* 'Family Life' column. Feedback came from huge numbers of readers who claimed that their husbands were 'exactly the same as Giles'. What did they mean? Well usually that their husbands too suffered from an inability to find things that were staring them in the face, from hypochondria, from the habit of blabbing out secrets they had sworn to keep in front of a table full of people (one of whom was often the actual subject of the secret), from a hatred of criticism, an insatiable appetite for praise, from tinpot dictatorism . . . It was the same all over the country.

Why are women so often attracted to men they will ultimately find maddening? 'Don't you know,' said my friend Louise's mother, 'that the strongest emotion in marriage is irritation?'

Ahead I provide reams of anecdotal evidence to give succour to the modern wife and consolation in the knowledge that she is not alone. And I recommend she stays put. Quite apart from the financial and administrative nightmare of changing to another man, and the appalling embarrassment of a new partner seeing you in the nude, trading one man in for another has rarely proved to have been worth it. Because, as I demonstrate, each man is *wildly annoying* in his own individual way.

MEN ABOUT
THE HOUSE

Time was when a woman's place was in the home. As she wiled away those happy hours in peace and contentment, she could look forward to the end of the day when her man would come back from toiling in the real world. How could she have ever dreamt that one day, dread of all dreads – a man's place would also be in the home?

On the day that he registered the birth of our second child my husband came unstuck when asked to name his occupation. Which occupation? When I married him he was a mosaicist. He then became a topographical artist but has since diversified into garden design and writing. The trouble with freelance artists, writers and landscape gardeners is that they can, theoretically, do much of their 'work' from home. Their numbers have now been supplemented by men who find that the new electronic possibilities of the age mean there is no reason why they should not run their businesses from home.

These men about the houses are putting out of joint the noses of wives who would occasionally like to get on with doing nothing without being supervised. We do not want our happy domestic trances perpetually broken. I recently read a perfectly plausible short story about a wife who, after thirty-three years of stable marriage, decided she had better file for divorce as her husband's retirement loomed. She couldn't face the idea of him hanging around the house – not least because he would finally find out how little she did with her own day.

I can easily identify with her on those days when the inclement weather hampers progress in my husband's two outdoor careers and we find ourselves rattling around the cottage together. Then I come under constant interrogation by a man who has adopted the persona of a part-time police officer.

'What are you doing now? Why hasn't such and such been done? Can I give you a bit of advice?' Even, waving a calendar once, an accusatory, 'I thought there were supposed to be four weeks in every month. Can you please explain to me why there are five Wednesdays in March?'

Susie's husband Mal is a landowner. She has therefore been obliged to accept that he will always 'work' from home.

'He regularly comes marching into the house like a commandant,' sighs Susie, 'sits down on the sofa with the remote control and zeroes on to Sky Sport. He then turns to me – I might be reading a book because the baby is asleep or something – and says "Haven't you anything better to do? Shouldn't you be getting on with writing thank you letters?" '

My friend Jo is a housebound mother of two little boys named Fred and William. At one stage in the recent past her art-dealing husband Gerry decided to operate from their home and so, after fifteen years of laughter and love-filled marriage which was entirely connected with his going to an office every day, Gerry too joined the ranks of home policemen.

'What are you doing now, Babe?' he would ask as he followed her about the house.

'Getting on with my life. What are you doing?'

'Oh I just like being with you, Babe, and seeing what you do with your day,' he would reply with a hint of censure in his voice.

Jo and I used to share an enjoyable addiction to talking to one another three or four times a day on the telephone. Just nuisance calls, as we openly referred to them, keeping up, soap opera–style, with minute developments in our own lives and those of others in our Venn diagrams. Suddenly this dependable pleasure was denied me as, after half a ring, Gerry would pick up the phone.

'Hello Mary, how can I help you?'

'Oh, is Jo there?'

'I think she's busy. Anything I can do?'

'Ah, no, it was just a nuisance call . . .' I would reply lamely before making the pointless request, 'Ask her to ring me when she's not busy.' Sometimes I did get through to Jo, but more often than not Gerry would pick up an extension and say something like, 'Sorry to interrupt, but can you come upstairs, Babe? William's got a felt tip.'

No wonder the wife of a building contractor I know has put her foot down and refused to let him set up office in their home. 'For better, for worse,' she tells her victimised girlfriends for whom it is already too late, 'but definitely never for lunch.'

HYPOCHONDRIA

'I'm feeling a bit odd, Babe,' I heard Jo's husband Gerry say to her one morning.

'Oh not again, Babe,' groaned Jo. 'What is it this time?'

'I don't know,' said Gerry slowly. 'All I know is that I just don't feel right. I've got this funny dull ache just behind my temples . . .'

Gerry's symptoms are always fairly non-specific and when urged to visit a doctor he likes to decline on the grounds that he will 'wait and see how this develops'. By the following day the first set of symptoms will have been superseded by another set, hinting at quite another condition altogether.

'Well the good news is that I think I've managed to fight off that flu I was starting to go down with yesterday. But now I've got the most terrible pain in my gut. It could be just simple indigestion from that disgusting restaurant we went to last night, but I've got a feeling it's something a bit more worrying. Ouch! There it is again. That was agony. You are looking at a man who may well be on his last legs. You'd better cancel dinner tonight, Babe.'

'And you'd better go to the doctor.'

'No. I think I'll give it a few hours and just see how it develops . . .'

In my own husband's case the hypochondria takes a slightly different form. While Gerry suffers from the ghosts of symptoms present, Giles looks forward to the ghosts of symptoms yet to come. 'I may look well but if you ask me it's too good to last. It'll be a miracle if I don't go down with a chronic infection after you let me get so cold yesterday by not insisting that I wore a warmer jersey when I went out into that biting wind.'

At the back of his mind Giles longs for invalidity as it has for him an unconscious association with happiness. As a boy, he suffered from asthma and spent many weeks in bed being bludgeoned with affection by his mother.

'One short tap on the floor with a walking stick would bring her up with a plate of soggy toast and Marmite,' he often reminisces nostalgically. 'Two taps would bring an orange peeled and segmented and laid out in the shape of a face.' He grew out of asthma but not before he had learned the simple equation that illness equals love and attention.

If the programme *Casualty* explores the world of mankind's serious ills, then Giles's life represents the imagined world of minor irritating complaints and medical 'own goals'. The own goals include burning his throat by drinking coffee when it is too hot and grazing the roof of his mouth on a biscuit.

One hot summer day I looked at him as he stalked manfully across our field, after an impressive two or three hours of back-breaking hole-digging and tree-planting. 'You're obviously really strong and fit,' I said, 'or you wouldn't have been able to do that labouring job.'

He looked far from pleased. 'But I think I've done too much. I've let myself get too tired.'

'Maybe. But at least you're not ill today.'

'No. This is the first day I've felt well for months, and do you know what the tragedy is? I've gone and bitten my tongue.'

'Clinical hunger' occurs at six pm, when a bag of crisps can restore his 'blood sugar level' to normal. This is also a time of wild mood swings leading to attacks of 'Tourette's Syndrome', where the patient is unable to control his foul language.

I think I may be going down with something.

'★★★★! I've let myself get too hungry.'

One good thing – I recently bought him the BMA handbook of home diagnosis, which he consults with great interest. He has found, while drinking instant coffee (a known mood alterer) that the 'permanent stye' on his lower eyelid is in fact a tear duct. One wrong self-diagnosis he made was of 'worms'. Our GP returned the result that the samples he had sent in were in fact loo paper.

Giles once visited the casualty ward of St Stephen's Hospital in London with a 'clinical sore throat'. He asked his doctor to perform a liver function test because he felt that his hangovers were worse than other people's. Is there a criminal charge of wasting a doctor's time?

Jo's friend Sarah has dealt with her husband's symptoms in a very efficient manner. James used to ring Sarah from the car to describe his symptoms and announce his imminent arrival at home where he would take to his bed. This was until Sarah introduced the new rule that he was simply not allowed to come home if he was ill. As a result he used to turn up at Jo's house, looking sheepish, which is how she found out about it. As far as I know James's symptoms abated soon afterwards.

Jo and I have had a measure of success with the symptom diaries we started keeping. We pass no comment but simply make detailed notes of our husbands' complaints over particularly bad periods. Then, every so often, we have a showdown.

> *Giles and Gerry*: 'There's something very, very badly wrong with me.'
> *Jo and Mary*: 'So, what's new? You're ill every day.'
> *Giles and Gerry*: 'No I'm not. I haven't been ill for months.'
> *Jo and Mary*: 'Yes you have,' (as we bring out the symptom diaries,) 'here's the evidence.'
> *Giles and Gerry*: 'Don't be daft. That was a joke. This time I really am going down with something.'

Once Giles came back home after three weeks in Kenya. Slim as a lath, brown as a berry and fit as a fiddle, he walked through the door.

'Well,' I said. 'You look incredible. For once you can't say you're going down with something.'

'No,' he said. 'I feel very well. The only thing is, I've got really bad Phantom Hat. You know, when you've been wearing a hat every day because of the sun and you keep thinking you've still got one on?'

His mother is still interested and sympathetic, though even she gets fed up with it sometimes.

'Oh well, darling,' she joked last time she came to stay, 'at least when you die we'll be able to put on your gravestone: "This time he really did go down with something".'

TRIGGERS FOR ARGUMENTS

To raise a laugh at dinner parties Cyril sometimes tells the story of his grandparents who lived alone in a bleak house on Dartmoor and argued their way through years of married life. One night, during dinner, they were arguing as usual when the grandfather left the long oak table, at which they sat at opposite ends, and stormed upstairs. Moments later there was a loud report and he staggered back into the dining-room, blood pouring from a gunshot wound. His last words were, 'Now look what you've made me do!'

Married couples usually react to this anecdote with nervous laughter. It is a bit close to the bone for those of us who indulge in squabbling on a daily basis. Yet there seem to be so many more potential triggers for arguments in today's complicated domestic life than there were for previous generations.

In my own household, for example, the fridge occasionally starts to fill up with water. Whose job is it to remember to 'periodically' clean a drainage hole at the back with a pipe-cleaner, as the instructions recommend? Each new machine seems to come with a similar catch: periodically remove this or that for cleaning purposes; do not allow temperature of room to rise above sixty degrees Fahrenheit; failure to empty the crumb tray will shorten the life of the toaster, etc. Modern conveniences provide a minefield of opportunities for blaming your co-habitee when they go wrong.

Then, the problem of tamper-proof packaging. It was bad enough trying to feed recalcitrant children with their *à la carte* tendencies before tamper-proof packaging came in. Now the whole process is much more time-consuming. Giles, wrestling with the interior sleeve of a Weetabix packet, shouted one morning, 'It's not paper and it's not polythene but it's strong enough to tow a car with!'

At that moment he found a fault-line along the seam of the sleeve and about six biscuits ejected themselves amid a flurry of crumbs. 'She won't eat these now. They're damaged,' he said gloomily. 'Life is becoming so difficult. Now you need a whole set of tools in every room just to open tamper-proof packages. I even have to carry garden shears in the car to cut open packets of batteries for the car torch. And any time left over from tempting the children to eat and cutting open tamper-proof packages,' he moaned, 'is spent in trying to get the baby seat into or out of our car and into or out of the nanny's car.'

Time was, of course, when you weren't jostling up against your husband all day because he used to be at work between nine and five. Now we have the territorial problem to add to everything else.

You might presume that couples who have lived together before marriage have an advantage over previous generations since the arrangement allows for the screening of potential partners for annoying habits or faults. My sister-in-law's flatmate at Essex University had a boyfriend who used to enjoy coming up behind her at the kitchen sink when she was washing up and manipulating her arms as though she were a rag doll. He thought this was hilarious – until he got the push. And a friend of ours terminated her liaison with an apparently god-like boyfriend when he used the word 'vehicle'.

But the weeding-out process is not always fool-proof. After a six-year courtship, my own husband developed a vibrato whistle the day we returned from our honeymoon in Crete. Shortly afterwards he also developed a high-pitched woman's yelp at the end of each yawn.

In his turn he says he didn't know what I was really like until we got married and he found that when I had flu I wanted the bedroom window open a crack at the same time as having the heater on. As I lie in bed suffering from my usual bi-annual dose of flu, Giles bursts into the bedroom five or six times a day to rage with genuine distress about the 'criminal waste of money heating the garden', but I croak back that I don't want to lie in a hermetically sealed germ bank all day.

Another habitual argument ensues each evening at dusk when he rushes towards the cottage curtains, knocking furniture aside in his eagerness to draw them.

'Don't shut out the lovely gloaming,' I beg.

'But there are people out there who might be tempted by the opulent furnishings.'

'What opulent furnishings?' I snap, as a glance around whatever room we are in will usually be enough to trigger dissatisfaction at the *lack* of opulence of the furnishings.

A Jungian analyst we know suggests that we complement each other and that we need each other to 'steer a middle course' to ensure harmony. Thus while my husband loves to 'purge the house of clutter' with a bonfire in the field while I am in London, I like to keep memorabilia in the form of papers and clothing, even though he claims they could retrigger his asthma attacks.

DOMESTIC CRIME
AND
PUNISHMENT

I am never surprised that *Crimewatch* is such a popular programme, and compulsory viewing for both criminals and law-abiders alike. Englishmen – and this is where Basil Fawlty rang so many bells – love a bit of amateur policing. What makes them very happy is to come home unexpectedly and catch their wives 'at' some petty crime, such as putting her feet up or talking on the phone at peak time.

'Such a wonderful thing has happened,' Susie told me on the telephone one morning (at peak time). 'We came home from a weekend at the Tollers' and Mal's keys were hanging in the lock. They'd been there all weekend,' she sighed in ecstasy. 'He would have given his eye teeth for them to have been my keys.'

Coming home for lunch exhausted from painting out of doors, pruning apple trees or laying a hedge, my own husband does not collapse in a chair with a pint of Goliath ale. Instead he goes directly to my office to check that the thermostat on my Dimplex heater is set at a minimum. On his way through the house towards it, his hands reach out octopus-like to switch off lights and central heating and to pour most of the water out of the recently filled kettle down the drain. 'No point heating up more than you need – it contributes to global warming.'

There is nothing warm about our cottage, which stands in the teeth of a permanent gale that sweeps up the plain towards it. A plain where only prostrate trees survive, although Giles has planted hundreds to shelter the house so as to save on heating bills (and to give him a chance to police the weeds at their base).

'You shouldn't need the heating on in November – what is going to happen when it's really cold?' he barks. 'People have forgotten how to dress warmly – jerseys, long-johns, vests, get them on!'

'I don't want to clad myself like a hot-water tank because if I do it means I can't move my arms. Then I can't use my word processor so that's not very efficient.'

Clad like a hot-
water tank.

'Everyone knows that if you want to keep warm in a cottage you've got to keep moving.'

He would like to police my purchases when I go to Waitrose but as he can't stand shopping I have to wait till later to receive a dressing-down for having bought the wrong things. Once I looked at our calendar to see he had written in my own section: 'Check what we have already got too much of. Then buy more of the same thing.'

One day Susie and I had a laugh. We went to the Early Learning Centre in Kensington and found there were baskets of flake-bar sized toy policemen made of a pleasing form of rubber. Susie bought one for her own husband and one for Giles. We were driving down to the country together and Giles positioned his on the dashboard, like a mascot, so he could admire it all the way to Wiltshire.

Yet Susie was soon laughing on the other side of her face as the motorway brings out the latent policeman in Giles like nothing else. Having passed a sign saying '50 mph mandatory speed limit', Giles switched to the fast lane and sat there at fifty miles per hour to stop others from exceeding the limit. This put us in as much danger as driving at speed on the hard shoulder would, with cars undertaking us and bearing down from all directions.

'Why don't you just join the police force?' I screamed in terror. 'Just give in to it! It's obviously what you want. And you'd get a salary.'

He looked sheepish. 'Can't I be an attendant in a public park instead?' he asked. 'I'd much rather tell off children for going on the flower beds than deal with frightening men with crowbars.'

MOTORWAY MISERY
AND THE CURE

If the world is a global village, Britain is a global street. In a way it is something of a disadvantage that we can now, theoretically, drive between one part of Britain and another with reasonable ease. Were it out of the question to go hundreds of miles for a weekend, as it used to be, many of us would probably be quite happy to stay at home.

Let's take a look at my husband's brother, whom Giles calls 'Little Pip Wood' despite the fact that Philip is twenty-nine. Pip, who is a 'little chartered surveyor', now has his 'own little life' and this means he is old enough for his social life to have become complicated. He has met and liked people at school, at university, at home, abroad and in London. He has therefore joined the ranks of those who spend each weekend on motorways, droning inexorably to and from far-flung corners of the country in a Sisyphean attempt to service all their friendships and family relationships.

One of the places where the cheery little chap regularly spends the weekend is the Lake District, to which he sets off with his bride Lois in a bid to visit her parents. 'We're going to the M6 for the weekend,' quips Pip. Seven-and-a-half hours spent getting there in nose-to-tail traffic on the Friday night means that Pip is so exhausted on arrival he has to sleep in till eleven on the Saturday morning to recover. He then has thirteen waking hours before going to bed again, this time at midnight. Rising again at ten on the Sunday morning, he has six waking hours before setting off for the drive back to London at four that afternoon.

This gives him a total of seventeen waking hours in the Lake District but fifteen waking hours spent getting there.

Like his older brother, Pip suffers from 'negorrhoea' during these marathon journeys – negorrhoea being an inability to stop being negative about the hellishness of the journey and, by keeping banging on about it, making it worse.

If a problem shared is supposed to be a problem halved, I have noticed the reverse is the case when the Wood brothers get together. Their negorrhoea then becomes greater than the sum of its parts. One weekend the four of us drove to Norfolk in the same car. Lois and I sat in the back trying to ignore the brothers as they competed to point out ugly buildings – 'That should never have got planning permission!' – or to complain about the traffic. 'This traffic is unbelievable,' they repeated time and again.

'There's only one thing worse than being stuck in traffic,' Lois said. 'Your attitude to being stuck in it.'

All the way to the motorway service station the brothers complained about the type of people they would expect to see there – 'I warn you, there will be some absolutely terrifying individuals there and what's more apparently one third of all people in any service station at any given time have gone there for a day out from somewhere local. They think it's a treat – that gives you an idea of what sort of people we're going to be seeing. But we're going to have to stop. We're too hungry not to,' said Pip.

'The worst thing about the service station is that the seats are screwed down so that you can't rock on them or push your chair back when you've finished eating and make a scraping noise,' said Giles. 'That spoils everything.'

Motorways engender a certain madness. A pit-stop mentality that encourages you to stay on the straight and, more often than not, narrow with so many contra-flows. This other world is often enlivened only by the sudden sighting of the 'motorway kestrel'. We had reached a rather beautiful stretch of the M11 and having run out of blots on the landscape to point out Giles announced, 'We're running very low on petrol and we're not actually going to make it to the service station because there isn't one for another forty-three miles. There's nothing I can do, this is absolutely terrifying. We're more or less driving to our doom.'

'Let's go off at the next exit then.'

'There's no point, because we won't know where the nearest garage is.'

'Well we can ask someone.'

'Yes, but none of us can follow directions. We know that.'

Pip nodded in grim agreement. 'Whenever we've stopped to ask directions Giles and I have always been too busy nodding at the person giving them to take in what they're saying.'

The fear and hysteria was mounting in the back seat and Lois and I seemed powerless to break into the brothers' trance of wilful impotence. Eventually, of course, we did come off the M11 at exit eight and asked a sequence of people, following their directions two sentences at a time, until we arrived at a garage.

The prospect of another hundred miles in a car with two sadists filled me with utter gloom but Lois had the answer. She came swaggering out of the garage shop with a virtual sack of Werther's Originals. 'Don't you know about sucky sweets?' she asked. 'I always have them in our car. Every time Philip opens his mouth to complain I pop one in.'

She was right. The Wood brothers sucked away in silence for the rest of the journey.

EATING
FOR TWO

In the two years since Giles and I visited a fashionable London nutritionist we have seen dramatic benefits from the eating programme she advised – when we stick to it. Gudrun told us to lay off certain foodstuffs to which she said we were sensitive (wheat, yeast, dairy products, etcetera) and which had induced in us the condition of 'toxic gut'. We were to adhere to a policy of eating starch and protein separately and whichever we chose to eat had to be accompanied by five times as much salad or vegetables. We should never eat more in volume than would fit into our cupped hands as, said Gudrun, this corresponded accurately to the natural size of our stomachs which should not be stretched by overloading.

Giles enjoyed the diet at first and particularly the interest and enquiries it excited amongst friends as the weight tumbled off him at a rate of knots until he weighed a *svelte* eleven stone.

Yet as the interest died down, it became clear that the food-combining diet had also provided him with a unique tool for drawing attention to himself when eating with friends, and he rather missed the beam of its spotlight. He soon found a way of encouraging its return.

For example. 'Oooh! Yorkshire pudding!' he will cheer. Then, calling across the table to me, 'Am I allowed that, Mary?' Turning to his neighbours, 'We're on this absurd diet and I never know what's allowed and what's not.'

Controlling the urge to rise to the bait I furrow my brow benignly and ask his neighbour, 'I'm not sure – what would you say? If we are not supposed to combine starch and protein can he have Yorkshire pudding with roast beef?'

'Definitely not!' the neighbour will laugh. 'Yorkshire pudding is made of flour, isn't it?'

To which Giles replies, 'Oooh, but it surely won't do me any harm just this once, Mary, will it? It's traditional to have Yorkshire with roast beef and I wouldn't want to offend my hostess by not having it.'

'Just have the beef with vegetables,' I mouth.

'Sorry, speak up Mary. What are you saying? I think it's rather bad manners to come to people's houses and start being neurotic about the food they are very kindly offering us, don't you?'

I give up.

As we drive home Giles will say, 'Why didn't you stop me from eating so much? I feel absolutely bloated now. You've really let me let myself down.'

'Because I'm not going to be drawn into a Punch and Judy show every time we have lunch with someone just so that you can be the centre of attention.'

'Well it's a pity you didn't stop me because I've eaten far, far too much and I think that lunch has definitely given me a virus so I'm going to be good for nothing for the next few days.'

As far as battles of will are concerned, it is all or nothing for Giles – and for his sister, who shares this family trait. Both are either spiralling downwards in a negative vortex of eating, drinking and time-wasting or they are spiralling upwards in a positive vortex of health and efficiency. But at

Easter, with cheeks bulging with Freya's chocolate eggs, he said to his mother, with whom we were staying, 'I'm afraid I'm in a negative spiral at the moment. It's all Granny's fault, of course.'

'Why on earth are you blaming her?' asked his mother in astonishment.

'Don't you remember how she always gave us chicken for Sunday lunch in the days when chicken was a treat? We used to see her going back into the kitchen and pulling off more and more strips of crispy after the table had been cleared. She used to encourage me to do it too.'

'Well, it's funny that her own daughter wasn't similarly affected,' I remarked. Giles's mother is as slim as a reed and a model of self-control. 'Anyway,' I went on, 'if you were so prepared to be influenced by your grandmother's example, it's funny you don't play bridge or golf or work as a consultant anaesthetist.'

Giles responded by inserting another mini-egg into his mouth. 'Why don't you just ignore me when you see me eating toxins?' he suggested. 'You are creating a tense atmosphere.'

Giles's mother, who is expert at defusing tension, yawned pleasantly as she admired Snowdonia from her conservatory window.

'Because,' I scowled, 'being Irish I express my emotions instead of bottling them up.'

'Actually Mary's right,' continued Giles, even prepared to turn against himself as long as he could prolong a conversation *about* himself. 'It's silly to spend so much money on a nutritionist and then ignore her advice about toxins.'

'I don't know why you had to go to a nutritionist,' said his mother. 'Couldn't you both just eat less piggy amounts?'

SHOPPING

As I am unable to drive I am at the mercy of a husband who will brook no dawdling in a Waitrose or other outlet for essential goods. I love shopping but he does not.

Parking (usually double-parking) outside our local Waitrose, he wears a 'patience of a saint' expression on his face. Often I can see his lips mouthing the words 'Come on! Come *on*!' as though his life were in danger and he were waiting to be plucked to safety by helicopter.

Our worst shopping row was in a lavatory shop in 1988. We had just moved into our new cottage and located the nearest bathroom equipment outlet thirty minutes away. As we walked through the door Giles spotted a lavatory with '£49.99' written on it. 'Come on,' he said. 'Let's get this one. There's nothing wrong with it.'

'But I want to go round the shop looking at all the others . . .'

'What difference could that possibly make? This one's only forty-nine ninety-nine and we haven't got all day. What's wrong with it?'

'Well, nothing immediately obvious, but it's not particularly nice and I think it's quite reasonable to say that if you're going to be using something six times a day possibly every day for the rest of your life, then it's worth taking a bit of time to choose one in a nice shape.'

'The assistant obviously thinks you're completely mad,' Giles hissed.

'Well,' I hissed back nastily. 'If she's reached the age of fifty and is selling lavatories for a living, I can't say I value her powers of judgement that highly.'

Perhaps one of the reasons why Giles hates shopping so much – apart from the parting with the cash – is that his own rare experiences of the activity have invariably been so negative. He was once traumatised by the reaction of a twenty-stone assistant in an ironmonger's shop in Battersea to whom he had made the innocent request, 'Two-and-a-half litres of Dulux white emulsion paint, please'.

'We don't sell rubbish here, mate,' replied the thug. 'Next customer.'

It turned out that they only sold their own (inferior) brand of paint. Since the incident Giles has always gone out of his way to avoid passing the shop when we go through Battersea on our way to friends in Balham.

As an inexperienced shopper he is also unused to the irritations and thwartings of a typical spree. For one who normally remains blissfully unaware of them they come as an outrage. While I was bed-bound in the tenth month of my last pregnancy Giles had to take charge of all shopping requirements, and his eyes were opened somewhat. At one trip to our local chemist he complained of finding a whole group of assistants 'swarming around a non-functioning till in slow motion' and ignoring him.

'Could someone serve me please!' he begged. 'I'm parked illegally.'

'Well I can't help that, sir,' retorted one of them.

'Do you have castor oil?'

'No,' she replied, pulling a face, according to him, as

though he had asked for a flask of urine. They no longer stocked castor oil and, warming to her theme, she came out from behind the counter to say that 'the only other place you might find it will be closed now'.

Shop assistants, he now believes, only get real job satisfaction when they can tell a customer they do not have the requested item. He also finds it mystifying when a shop-keeper says: 'We do have it but it's not in stock.'

'Why can't they just tell the truth?' says Giles. 'They don't have it there and then and that's when you want it.'

Often he will leave the engine running when he drops me at Waitrose and parks outside. This is foolhardy, as the shortest possible time it could take me would be seven minutes and the more likely average time is thirty. Once I get back into the·car he roars home bitterly.

'Now I insist on being allowed to go into the garden to make the most of what's left of the day,' he says.

'All right then,' I retort. 'Let's not go shopping again. Let's do without food and drink, light bulbs and loo paper!'

'There's no need to be aggressive,' he reasons. 'I just don't see why you have to take so long. I could do the shopping in a quarter of the time because I don't waste hours picking things up, staring at them in a trance and then putting them down again.'

And though I could say 'Why don't you do the shopping then?' of course I do not. How could I willingly deprive myself of the guaranteed rush of pleasure that comes from handling shiny new goods and having the money to put them in my basket and pay for them?

SUCKING
UP TO
WORKMEN

'Giles?' I said, tentatively. I knew he was just around the corner, mulching. I was sitting in the garden feeding the baby her breakfast of banana and longing for a cup of tea myself but feeling too faint to make it.

'Giles?' I called again as there was no response. Funny, I was sure he was only literally about seven paces away. 'Giles,' I said in a louder voice. 'Giles, Giles, Giles, Giles, Giles.' Suddenly he sprang from behind the wall.

'Why do you keep calling me in that hysterical way?'

'Well if you knew I was calling, why didn't you answer the first time?'

'What do you want?' he whined. 'I'm in the middle of a project.'

'I'm feeling really faint, and all the health experts say a woman who has just had a baby needs to be cosseted and to rest the whole time, so could you make me a cup of tea?'

'All right, I'll make you a cup of tea!' He strolled past me saying loudly, 'Women! Strewth!' rolling his eyes and shaking his head in an uncharacteristic manner.

Women? Strewth? He's never used either of those expressions before, I thought . . . then I remembered. There were workmen on the premises. The performance was for their benefit.

My husband always turns quisling when workmen come into our cottage. Pretending to be an Ordinary Bloke, he sides with them against me in disputes over what we need to have done and how soon they are going to do it. Two men had come to fit a stereo radio tuner and aerial: the aerial was necessary, they said, as our cottage in the Wiltshire Downs falls outside the normal pick-up range for Radio 3.

Workmen, I have noticed, like to patronise a woman in her home. I, however, adopt a schoolmistress persona when dealing with them in an attempt to ensure we are neither duped nor left with a bungled job. 'Can you just fit the tuner first, without the aerial?' I had asked, determined we should not pay more than was necessary. 'I was listening to Radio 3 the other day and it really didn't seem too bad. Let's just hear what it sounds like without the aerial first.'

The men's faces were contemptuous and Giles's followed suit. As it turned out we really did need the aerial. The men fitted it, and an hour after they arrived Giles burst anxiously into my office interrupting an important call and gesticulating wildly. 'Come on! Come on! We have to decide on the cheap tuner or the middling one. Come now. Mr Brown is waiting.'

'So?' I hissed. 'He can't be in that much of a hurry.'

A particularly strident passage – from Mahler's Fifth, as it turned out – was blaring forth as I came into the room. The men were gazing alternately at the ceiling and the floor with impatience.

'Are you sure that's Classic FM?' I laughed. 'It sounds more like Billy Smart's Circus.'

Giles and the workmen rolled their eyes at one another in an exchange of 'I give up' glances.

We switched to Radio 3.

'There's a crackle!' I pointed out.

Giles shook his head firmly as though I were clearly mad, but, to my delight, Mr Brown said: 'Yes, there is a crackle, but I think they're playing an old record . . .'

'Well, it's a good sound,' I said magnanimously. 'Let's have this tuner then. And can I have a butterfly clip to improve the reception on my radio in the office?'

'I thought you said it was all right,' jeered Mr Brown.

By now Giles had switched sides completely. Sighing heavily, he spoke slowly, as if addressing a child. 'But if we had known you wanted one of those two hours ago, Mary, we would have installed the aerial on a different wall, wouldn't we?'

'I'm afraid your husband's right,' said the workman. Giles continued tutting and rolling his eyes. 'You should have trusted the professionals to tell you what you needed in the first place,' he said, nodding sagely towards them. 'In my own family we always did that.'

'Hang on a minute,' I said, drawing myself up to my full width. 'You seem to have forgotten something. This *is* your own family.'

NANNY
KNOWS
BEST

During the reign of Mrs Thatcher it was sometimes observed that many of our leading Conservative politicians had been brought up by strict and scolding nannies. This factor, it was conjectured, explained their subjugation to the Iron Lady.

The great British Nanny, as celebrated in Jonathan Gathorne-Hardy's classic study of 1972, may now be under threat from Australian invaders, but the Englishman's appetite for a relationship with a nagging and bossy woman is still evident throughout the classes from Prince Andrew to Andy Capp. For a man it is quite reassuring to have a reliable source of nagging in his life. Someone is taking an interest in me, says the unconscious, someone is holding the reins and will snatch me back in time. What fun is there in doing only things you're allowed to do? None. Far, far more fun and feeling of self-importance if an authority figure in the form of a grown-up woman is worrying at the sidelines. But what grown-up woman is going to care whether you do naughty or dangerous things? Only the woman with a vested interest in your well-being, your girlfriend or wife.

'Gerry hates being nagged,' his wife told me, 'But his doctor said he had the cholesterol levels of a fifty-year-old and he was heading for trouble. So I started him on a diet on Monday and he's been really sticking to it.'

Old Etonian Gerry's food abuse is a legend amongst the generally thin and elegant London sophisticates who make up his circle. His popularity is by no means diminished by his Buddha-like physique, nor by his public consumption of huge amounts of unhealthy foodstuffs – the vicarious pleasure given by this 'Elvising' could never be underestimated and, as Princess Elizabeth Bibesco once wrote, 'How much easier to make pets of our friends' weaknesses than to put up with their virtues.'

'Gerry's got bulimia without the vomiting!' one friend quipped.

'Now he has cottage cheese and sweetcorn for lunch,' Jo was telling me when we heard the front door unexpectedly slam. Tiny (heightwise) and bespectacled Gerry entered the room. Stripping down to his underpants as he came through the door, he made his way to the kitchen leaving a trail of clothes in his wake. First to the bread bin where he helped himself to a loaf of Mother's Pride. Then to an area of the carpet directly in front of the television set where he sat down with a double-decker sandwich filled with butter (the same width as the bread itself), baked beans, cheese and mayonnaise, all topped off nicely with a layer of potato crisps. There he sat silently gorging, a litre of Diet Coke by his side, a magazine to catch the drips.

For a moment Jo studied him in silent horror. Then she said, 'Gerry, what would you do if I left you?'

'Then I'd change my ways, Babe,' said Gerry, hugging himself childishly, 'and be really good and nice until I got you back.'

Jo decided to give up on his diet, as she had done so many times before. 'He always said that his mother nagged him so much about over-eating that it just made him eat more,' she told me, with the placid acceptance that the sins of the mother simply will be visited on the wife.

But if you, reader, were or are a man and if you were Gerry, brought up by a nanny, and had had a verbal warning from your doctor, would you prefer your wife to smile on unreproachfully as you 'Elvised' or would you prefer her to be stricter with you? Wouldn't it feel better if she just came forward and took the toxins from you and sent you up to bed without any supper at all until you had apologised, where-upon she would let you have a light supper of consommé and dry toast followed by fruit? Yes it would, wouldn't it? And that was very obviously what Gerry was hoping Jo would do.

The trouble with being a nanny substitute, however, is that although some men, such as those in Mrs Thatcher's cabinet, want to please nanny, there are many other men who don't want to please nanny in the shape of mother, wife or boss. They rather want to bait her.

Take William for example. Go-ahead young man, *circa* thirty, works in the Foreign Office, married to Lizzie who, significantly, was head girl of her school, and maintains a fairly bossy stance towards William. 'Finish your sentences!' she snapped at him one night, in front of a surprised dinner party audience.

Lizzie and I were in the communal changing-room of Miss Selfridge one day when I noticed a red weal on her hip.

'How did you get that mark, Lizzie?' I asked.

William, it seemed, had been promising for eighteen months to move the heavy oak bed in which they slept in a room too small for it. It was meant to be a temporary measure as the room the right size for the bed was ceiling-high with boxes of William's possessions, which had been there since they moved in following their marriage those eighteen months before and were still waiting for William to unpack them.

Every night, when Lizzie had her bath and tried to pass between the space at the end of the bed and the radiator, she found she had to drop the towel to get through. Sometimes she made it through without burning her hip. More often than not she burnt it. Almost every night she gave William a dressing-down about not having moved the bed but their hectic social schedule meant that William somehow never had time, just after the argument, to do anything about it.

I saw William a couple of weeks after I had first seen the burn. 'Have you moved the bed yet?' I teased.

'No,' he replied, grinning with pleasure.

Now what sort of man would *want* to annoy his wife?

A friend of my parents died at the relatively early age of fifty-two. Why had he died so young, I asked my mother.

'Oh, he was just a typical man,' she sighed. 'All through his life he had a weak chest: his wife begged him and begged him not to keep going out to the garage without a coat in the bitterly cold weather but he wouldn't take any notice.'

Why is the woman's role so often that of the uphill struggler – desperately trying to stop men doing what both of us know will not be good for them? Why do we have to beg and beg them to claim their expenses, change out of their best suede brogues before gardening, remove their bulging wallets from their back trouser pockets before they go to the Notting Hill Carnival?

Because men *like* being nagged.

THE REAL
COST OF
DIY

Conrad, the carpenter whom I had asked to build some shelves for us, put his head around the door one morning to say he was sorry he had not been along for a bit but he was moving house.

'It's all right,' I said bitterly, 'providing it's not too long until you come back. I know I only asked you to do the shelves a few weeks ago but it's been six years since I've wanted them done . . .'

Conrad's serene face lit up. 'We've been in our place twenty-two years, and it's still not finished.

'My brother's the same,' he chuckled. 'He's a builder and he took two years off to work solidly on his own place, and it's nowhere near finished. A house is never finished.'

The thought that our tiny cottage might still be unfinished in fourteen years time gave me quite a bad adrenalin rush. Eight years ago, when we moved in, Giles was determined to do the restoration himself. He spent nearly one year patching up four rotten windows with car-body filler.

'How much would it cost to have proper replacement windows fitted?' I used to plead, as the 'restoration' proceeded at a snail's pace.

'No, no, no ... you don't want to start replacing windows,' Giles would reply witheringly. 'Creaking gates last longest. This sort of old wood is properly hung and seasoned. You can't get wood like it nowadays.'

The next year he painted the inside of the house and all the surfaces had to be rubbed down by hand with sandpaper. This meant that each room precipitated a protracted period of tool-downing as he had 'given myself asthma because of the dust. I'd better work in the garden for a few days'.

If the average Briton's wage during 1988 and 1989 was £12,000 a year, this meant that by repairing the windows and painting the walls himself, Giles had actually lost out on £22,000, i.e. £24,000 minus the £2,000 it would have cost to pay a workman to do it.

Yet, like many others at the time, he felt that the very fact of his ownership of this property meant that he was generating a fabulous, if abstract, sum each week. And if the property was being improved as well, then he was earning far, far more than he would be in a job. And, as he pointed out, real workmen were impossible to pin down anyway as they had all taken on more work than they could manage.

So he continued with his painstaking task. 'The reason it's taking me so long is because I'm a perfectionist. I won't do things in half measures. And all the time I'm adding to the value of the property.'

'But there's no point in adding to its value unless we're actually going to sell it, and we're not,' I used to reason. Yet there was also a prevailing ethos at the time that somehow your personal worth went up in direct proportion to the worth of your house.

Thank heaven for small mercies. The very dimensions of the cottage made it impossible for Giles to continue with his DIY for twenty-two years, and anyway he suddenly lost his taste for perfectionism one day when the estate agent brother of a friend came to lunch and Giles invited him to put a price on the cottage. Giles was surprised at the modesty of the figure. 'Yes,' said the estate agent, 'but what you've got to realise is that a lot of people would have to take into account the cost of completely gutting and redecorating the place which they would have to add on to the asking figure.'

Shortly afterwards Giles didn't put up that much resistance when I presented him with the *fait accompli* that while we were away on holiday in Norfolk one summer, a 'proper workman' was going to come into the house and finish up all the painting that still needed to be done.

BIRTH?
IT'S NO MAN'S
LAND

My husband claimed that he had been traumatised by witnessing the birth of our first child and would therefore prefer not to act as midhusband to the birth of our second – unless I was adamant or emotional.

'No man should have to undergo the experience of delivery,' he declared.

'No man does,' I replied coldly.

The more he talked about it the more Giles felt that he was in the vanguard of a new movement to liberate men from the tyranny of the delivery room and restore them to their rightful domain – the corridor or, even better, the home.

'For millennia,' he said, 'men have naturally regarded childbirth as women's business. Why should it suddenly change in the last twenty years?' To add weight to his theory he quoted his uncle Donald: 'In the wild, you see, a male tiger or lion might devour its young, and the mother instinctively knows that she should keep herself and her newborn cubs out of his way.'

'It's not a particularly apt analogy,' I said, but I determined to take him at his word. As he says, perhaps the fashion for husbands to ape midwives will in the future be regarded as a temporary blip, an historical aberration, like land girls. But a generation of men has now attended births, indeed some have proved themselves useful for timing contractions, doing breathing exercises, for giving emotional support or taking flak. Some wives actually want their husbands to be present, but I was more than happy to have with me the esteemed 'birth veteran' Betty Parsons, who has taught 30,000 mothers to 'relax for childbirth and for life'.

When the day for inducement came Giles became rather dog-in-the-manger-like. 'I don't want to find that I've boxed myself into a position where I can't even be present at my own child's birth,' he complained, his mouth pursing like a Venus flytrap.

'Well, you can come if you want,' I said. 'Leave your options open.'

All three of us arrived at the hospital for induction. Seventy-eight-year-old Betty and I were calm. Giles, on the other hand, within minutes of entering the hospital, took on a deathly pallor and a wild stare. 'You know hospitals have this effect on me,' he said. 'It's the smell and the noise.'

'Well, why don't you go into Oxford and have some lunch then, while we settle in?' I suggested. He agreed.

An avid supporter of park-and-ride schemes, he then drove several miles out of Oxford to the park-and-ride terminus even though the hospital itself was only minutes from the centre and had its own convenient bus service into town. On his return Giles stared out at the brown Oxford suburbs from our seventh-floor window and complained, 'That Indian meal I had is weighing very heavily on my stomach.'

'Why don't you go home and get some sleep?' suggested Betty. 'We will ring you once things start happening.'

'Then you can still come back in time to witness the highlights,' I added.

Well, as Betty had promised, the only predictable thing about labour is that it is entirely unpredictable and this one lasted only two-and-a-half hours. Conditions afforded no interval where anyone could have telephoned the reluctant midhusband to command his return. It was the best of all possible scenarios: Giles had not been there, yet it was not his 'fault' that he was not. Summoned at six am, he arrived quickly back at the hospital. Bursting into the room, he looked at his new daughter lying in her glass crib then, on my urging, picked her up and held her as though a workman had asked him to hold the other end of a plank for a few minutes. He still looked shaken, like a glove puppet without the hand in it. 'All this stress and strain is taking its toll on me,' he said. 'Have you got any effervescent vitamin C?'

The following day I beamed into my answering machine and picked up a conversation which had been recorded between Giles and his farmer friend, Desmond, from Norfolk. 'I didn't attend the birth,' Giles said sheepishly.

'Quite right,' barked Desmond. 'No need to. You can see plenty of pictures in the colour supplements.'

SO MUCH TO DO, NO TIME TO SAY WHAT

'Mummy, do you like Daddy?' asked Freya.

I must admit the question caught me off guard. 'Of course I like him. After all, I married him, didn't I!' I said.

Whether I actually like my husband is not something I have given much consideration to over recent years. Like the Inuit, we are locked into a daily struggle just to survive, and then a nightly struggle to get our children to sleep. These struggles leave very little spare time for being able to see the wood for the trees.

'Don't you resent your children taking up most of your evening as well as most of your day?' enquired Giles's younger brother, Pip, when he stayed for the weekend. Pip and his wife of two years have no children yet.

Giles had just sunk into an armchair with a bowl of stress-reducing corn tortillas. 'You just wait, Pip! Rocking a baby for thirty-five minutes every night is a lot less painful than finding time to read *Solve Your Child's Sleep Problems*. I am stuck on the chapter about sleep patterns and brainwaves. It's too technical.'

'But,' I interrupted, 'it says you can skip that chapter and then go back to it when you've finished the book.'

'Oh, I don't think we'll bother,' said Giles. 'The days go by so quickly they'll be at university soon. I can't see myself having four hours spare to finish reading the book before then.'

'I suppose,' said little Pip thoughtfully, 'that your life, biologically speaking, is over once you've had children? Apart from nurturing the new life, you are superfluous – just a link in the chain.'

'Yes,' sighed Giles. 'We've had our lives now.'

Pip laughed politely. 'But when do you and Mary get time for yourselves?' he asked.

Giles looked puzzled for a moment. 'The one time we used to be able to talk was when we were driving to and from Waitrose and we were alone in the car together. That was before Mary got a mobile phone. Now I can never get her attention,' he said gloomily. 'The other day one of her old French friends came to stay. She hadn't seen Mary for ten years and she asked her what had drawn her to this part of the country. Mary handed her an article from *Country Living* and said, "You can read that. I am too busy to tell you myself." Her friend said, "I don't want to read an article about it. I want you to tell me." Still, they're the best years of our lives. Aren't they, Mary?'

'Never clap me on the back!' I snapped. 'Why didn't you tell me that you hadn't put the chicken in the oven?'

'Aha!' crowed Giles. 'I did. But you had earplugs in so you've only yourself to blame. That means we won't be eating until midnight – again.'

'Oh, don't worry, we like eating at midnight,' said Pip's wife, Lois, diplomatically. 'But why was Mary wearing earplugs?'

'She has started wearing earplugs so that she can't hear my point of view if she thinks it's going to differ from hers,' said Giles. 'In one crude gesture she is rejecting civilised and

reasoned discussion in favour of a new post-feminist Nean-
derthalism.'

*She has started
wearing earplugs.*

Before going to bed, Pip and Lois were surprised to
witness a rare display of marital unity. We were watching the
televised news of the break-up of a celebrity marriage. 'It's
pathetic,' we shouted. 'Haven't they heard of working at
their marriage? What about the children? How could they do
it?'

'It could never happen to us,' said Giles cheerfully.

'Why not?' asked Pip, nervously.

'Because,' said Giles, 'if we can't find the time to discuss
our marriage, there will be even less time to discuss a
divorce. And what's the point of splitting up? If the days
carry on going by as quickly as this we'll be dead soon
anyway.'

PYRRHIC
PACKING

'If we don't get off now there'll be no point in going!' shouted Giles, Basil Fawlty-like, as he stood in the door-frame of our tiny cottage, marshalling a group of friends outside. 'Duck or grouse!' he shouted as they banged their heads. It was a Sunday afternoon; we had had our lunch. Now, 'Let's grab what we can of what's left of the day!' said Giles, managing to inspire joy and depression in the same short sentence.

But departure, even on a simple walk setting out from our cottage into the immediate environs, is always hindered by the sheer amount of 'packing' to be done in preparation. To and from their glove compartments and suitcases the guests rushed, looking for hats, gloves, scarves, mints, tissues, binoculars, cameras, lip salves, dog leads and sunglasses. 'Well, the day's virtually gone now,' said Giles twenty or so minutes later as he eventually started to lead the party through the clammy fog of a typical Sunday afternoon in March.

Having just had a baby I found it incredible to think that, given the difficulties of getting off on a walk, we had been in the habit of regularly spending whole weekends away. If the packing for these was complex, imagine how much more so it was going to be with the paraphernalia required by a newborn, I worried. The problem was that we were not just due to go off for a weekend, but off for a full holiday in a tropical country. I felt utterly daunted. Through a wave of freakish fortune we were to fly to Barbados to attend the Easter Opera Festival there. Our baby would be six weeks old as we boarded the plane.

Basil Fawlty's persona manifested itself again as Giles began packing eight days before the date of departure. I found him laying things out on our bed in neat piles while the window-sill was ranked with pharmaceutical products. He was already talking, in the clipped quasi-military tones that he adopts before embarking on long journeys, about his 'kit' and its lamentable state. 'Don't women darn socks any more?' and 'Who's responsible for not having sewn on these buttons?'

For most of the year Giles is proud of looking like a gardener or artist, but, when abroad, he becomes ultra-smart and urbane. This David Nivenisation probably began when he saw a young fellow-Briton in a Venetian church wearing a T-shirt saying 'Too drunk to f***'. Now, especially in international airports, he likes to dress well and be a good ambassador for his country.

'I'm travelling light again this year. How about you?' he asked nastily, knowing that I always pack too much and that, inevitably, I will be 'scattering' as my hand baggage always becomes unmanageable in its volume.

Scattering usually happens at a key moment in a pulsating crowd before boarding the plane. This involves the initial splitting open of a bag and then smaller containers hitting the ground. These, on impact, often burst open themselves, scattering even smaller containers of money, buttons, beads or felt-tip pens.

Giles, on the other hand, has a daily ritual of paring down the items in his case to such an extent that the goal of having the right 'kit' on arrival is usually sacrificed for the Pyrrhic triumph of having travelled light. Travel phobia runs in his family. Godfrey Wood, Giles's father, was known to actually *rehearse* packing a month in advance. 'It is linked in both of our minds to a fear of leaving our houses, rather like hermit crabs,' says Giles unconvincingly.

My greatest fear was that I would become separated from the others in my state of reduced mental capacity. Giles shared this fear with me and suggested that he keep me on a pair of retractable toddler's reins. I, normally cock-snooking, felt nervous as I tried to visualise how we would possibly manage all the luggage plus Moses basket, plus babe-in-arms and child-in-hand while my bags burst open around me.

It was at that moment that I felt the most intense envy of my friend Henrietta as the memory of her wedding came vividly into my mind. Henrietta had married a multi-millionaire and was in her going-away outfit and making the final touches to her packing before 'getting off' on her honeymoon to Venice. Her millionaire husband came into the room. 'Hurry up, Henrietta,' he said. 'There's no need to pack. You can buy everything you need when we get there.'

TABLE
MANNERS

When a friend of mine was fourteen and attending Holland Park Comprehensive School in the 1970s, her libertarian mother was hoist by her own petard. How could she stop her daughter from going out with appallingly unsuitable boys and, worse, possibly going to bed with them? As they were an irreligious family no rules of chastity could be applied so instead she appealed to her daughter's sense of vaingloriousness. 'But darling, it won't be worth it in the long run. Because if you go out with Tom it will mean that you won't be able to marry Prince Charles and become Queen when you get older.'

My own mother's approach was more realistic. 'There's nothing wrong with anyone from a different walk of life to your own and you can go out with boys from any walk of life,' she allowed magnanimously, 'but no one should ever marry someone from outside their own sort of background. If they do then they drive each other mad with the two different sets of table manners. Eating together three times a day, day after day, year after year ...' she shuddered eloquently.

Some women don't mind if men eat with their mouths

open, slurp their drinks noisily, commit other atrocities at the table. I am one of those who do, though I am happy to say that in this instance my own husband only offends when he remembers to.

Cyril, on the other hand, is one of the leading exponents of 'roving trotters'. This occurs when one of those sitting around a table plucks key nuggets of food from a central serving dish while the table is still being prepared around them. Such people often have the nerve to cry 'Mmmm!' in complimentary tones as they gobble down, for example, the only crispy bits in a salad or the only crispy parsnips.

Then there is RSA or Repetitive Smearing Action, where a party's fork is loaded and, to add flavour, existing food matter on his or her knife is applied with an excessive number of strokes.

Funnily enough, the chief offenders tend not to hail from my own walk of life but from the very top ranks of the social scale. There, an innate sense of superiority seems to preclude inhibition and crimes of a more striking nature can be witnessed.

Ambrose, aged thirty-two, is the son of a Marquess yet his table manners are even more 'Greystoke' than were those of Christopher Lambert when he took the part of the seventh earl in Hugh Hudson's film of Tarzan. Once returned from the jungle to his ancestral stately home we saw him horrifying society with his bestial eating methods. Once we invited Ambrose (six foot four and thirteen stone) to lunch and, as a joke, cooked two chickens instead of one. The first one we carved, the second we put on to Ambrose's plate in its entirety. Ambrose, who often helps himself absentmind-edly from the plates of those sitting close to him, showed no kind of surprise, nor did he laugh. 'Cor,' he said, 'is this all for me? Great!' before tackling the whole bird and finishing it.

As we were waiting for our second baby to be born my

husband, daughter and I spent Christmas alone in our cottage and made no social arrangements for family to join us. Yet faced with the fact that we had a ten-pound turkey to eat all on our own, with neither of us wanting to eat more than a pound of it, Giles had a brainwave. Ambrose and his mother were coming to spend Christmas Eve with us on their way through Wiltshire to their own house in Dorset.

'I've had a brilliant idea,' said Giles. 'Let's cook the turkey on Christmas Eve, then we can have the satisfaction of watching Ambrose eat most of it.'

Ambrose and Ann arrived from London at eight o'clock and between then and nine, Ambrose managed to cram about thirty roasted chestnuts and two bags of crisps into his six-foot-four-inched frame.

'Is it nearly ready?' he asked me impatiently at nine o'clock.

'Yes,' I replied. 'I'm glad you're still hungry.'

'I'm not that hungry,' said Ambrose dreamily. 'I just want to get the meal over and done with so I can lie on the sofa and watch telly.'

Why do I mind so much? No doubt, just as one over-reacts with indignation and denial to criticisms that one secretly knows to be valid, the real problem is that I too would like to be plucking key nuggets of crispy bits from central platters, slurping drinks noisily and lying back on sofas watching television, having bolted my food.

Only the restrictions inherent in hailing from my own middle-ranking walk of life prevent me from doing so.

LIGHTENING
THE LOAD
I

Fifteen was the number of our house party in Suffolk one week in the summer of 1994. Our magnanimous friend Cyril had taken the House in the Clouds, a rentable former water-tower near Aldeburgh, one hundred feet tall and a paradise for children.

A paradise for adults as well. At least this adult who finds family life much easier when not in her own home and when the squalor that is building up around her can not be solely her own responsibility.

The convenience of sharing a taste in friends should not be underestimated. Fortunately, Cyril and Giles seem to get along almost as well as Cyril, who gave me away at my wedding, and I. Yet whenever adult male primates are under the same roof an inevitable power struggle seems to ensue. Cyril, who earns £200,000 a year as a writer, is often rather tetchy due to the high pressure of his work.

It was he who once advanced the theory that friendship is often to do with subconsciously identifying 'equals' and then competing with them.

'Shall I tell you what the plan is?' asked an unusually genial Cyril one morning, addressing the breakfast table in general and the three other adult males in particular. 'We're all taking a boat on the Meare and we're going to have a picnic lunch there.' Anticipating mutiny he added: 'And that includes you, Giles. This isn't a country club you know.'

'Just let me know exactly what you intend to do, Cyril, and I'm sure I can work around it,' said Giles provocatively.

With the whole party packed into one tiny rowing boat, we lay low in the shallow Meare. Giles and Cyril were making a show of rowing as a team but there was an ongoing tussle as to who was stroke. Meanwhile Desmond offered to call out the rhythm.

'We'd better cut our losses, have a picnic right here in the boat and abandon your original plan,' said Giles to Cyril, goading him as he sat stationary above the mud, his arms exhausted. Cyril ordered Giles to the bow of the boat for his own safety. This redistributed the weight, enabling us to float off the mud bank and proceed to the island of Cyril's choice where we were bitten so badly by mosquitoes that two of us needed antihistamines later.

'Typical of Cyril not to know there would be mosquitoes along that slimy channel,' said Giles. 'If only he'd listened to me, it was obvious we should have stopped where there was a breeze.'

'Right,' said Cyril on Sunday morning. 'Who wants to go for a walk? I'm setting off in five minutes. Anyone who's not ready, we're going without them.'

Five minutes later Cyril was fuming. 'At any given minute you'll find there are five people who have said they are on for a walk and two of them can't be found and one of them is saying, "Oh, wait a minute, I've just got to do something." You have to be schoolmasterly about this sort of thing. Come on! And where's Giles?'

'Here I am,' said Giles. 'I've just been for a walk.'

'Well, thanks for asking me,' said Cyril.

'Oh, don't you know about going for a walk?' said Giles

loftily. 'I've learned from experience that there's no point in consulting anyone else about it or you never get off.'

The worst power struggles, however, were over who would cook the barbecue on the one really sunny barbecuey day. 'It's a seriously primeval thing,' laughed Desmond. 'It's about fire and it's about meat. Everyone thinks a barbecue must be a democratic thing but actually the man who ends up cooking the barbecue really is the dominant male of this pack.'

'What about the man who bought the barbecue?' chipped in Cyril, who had paid for the ingredients.

An hour later I came down from my room. 'So, the barbecue looks wonderful. Who ended up cooking it?'

'I did,' said Kate, the only single parent present. 'They were all so busy talking about who was going to do it and the children were getting really hungry so I just got on and did it. Single parents are the new men,' she said, as the pack of male primates hovered over the grill, jostling for the choicest protein nuggets according to their still-to-be-decided pecking order.

LIGHTENING
THE LOAD
II

'You can move in any time as far as I'm concerned,' boomed seventy-one-year-old Euan after a convivial dinner at Fogview, his ochre Gothic farmhouse on the hill.

'I think it might be a good idea,' Giles boomed back without hesitation. 'We'll come up at the first opportunity in January.'

Jo Farrell rang as we were packing the car up for our first night at Fogview. 'Are you sure it wasn't the drink talking when he invited you? Isn't your own house much nearer to Freya's school? What's in it for Euan?' she quizzed, coming straight to the point.

'Well he seems to actually enjoy our company, even Giles's,' I explained. 'We enjoy his company and he hates living alone in a huge house. We can each have our own room and it's a horrible time of year.'

'You'd better not spread your things all over his surfaces,' she warned.

Yet a week later, on the eve of moving back to our cottage, the only disharmony to occur arose when Giles complained that some butter was rancid.

'It's that word "rancid" that I object to,' drawled Euan.

52

'It's rather like the word "moist". Couldn't you have just said "I think this butter's slightly orff . . ."?'

It wasn't the last time that he would point out in a benign and avuncular way that there might be room for improvement in Giles's manners. And Giles was genuinely keen to imbibe from Euan's distillation of wisdom accrued over a lifetime of courtesy. 'I notice that you always stand up when Mary goes into or out of the room,' said Giles. 'Is it absolutely necessary for me to do it like a jack-in-the-box?'

'My dear fellow, at the very least you should shuffle in your seat as if intending to rise,' he commanded, adding 'Women, particularly wives, like it.'

I was naturally keen to encourage this instructive relationship. Yet I was to find that Euan has strong opinions on almost every aspect of life, no matter how banal, and that not all of his dictates are necessarily practical for harassed parents in the late twentieth century.

One day, for instance, Giles and Euan came back from a shopping trip to Gateways in Calne without some of the goods I had requested. 'Euan wouldn't allow me to take a trolley,' said Giles passively, 'so I couldn't fit everything into the basket.'

'No, it won't do,' said Euan. 'A bulging trolley looks so frightful. You must mince through the aisles with a basket, never taking any more than five items. If you need more than five then you may take two baskets. A gentleman never uses a trolley.'

'But it will waste time going in every day,' I reasoned.

'My dear girl, at seventy-one the main problem of my life is how to fill in time. I shall now go out again to the post office to waste time queueing for my pension and, with any luck, by the time I've finished it will be time for a large gin and tonic before luncheon.'

The week passed happily, Giles and I each working in our own room and, having colonised a whole corridor of the house like field mice, activities naturally expanded to fill the numbers of rooms available and the children played musical beds. We would meet at luncheon to discuss the logistical problems, one of the most involved of which was raised by a dinner invitation from the Sandersons, who live a furlong away from our cottage.

Three reasonably intelligent adults could not resolve such multiple-choice questions as were presented by this invitation. The main bone of contention was whether we should sleep in our own cottage after the dinner or make a round trip of twenty-four miles to sleep back at Fogview.

'Please stop discussing it,' I begged. 'I've got arrangement fatigue. Just make your minds up.'

'No,' boomed Giles, in Euan's voice, 'conversations such as these are hugely enjoyable. It's like worrying at a bone.'

The undoubted advantages of having much more space to lead our lives in was partly offset by having to refer all problems to a working party and thence to a committee for consideration and inevitably resulted in delay in taking even minor decisions.

'But,' said Euan, 'one wants to spin these things out. When you get to my age, discussing these complex arrangements fill up one's day rather agreeably.'

May I recommend to couples, however, that the temporary presence of a mutually compatible third party can bring joy, and a certain amount of relief into a marriage. As Alexandre Dumas fils had it, 'The chains of marriage are so heavy that it takes two to bear them, and sometimes three.'

END OF
EMPIRE

'That's right! Put some vim and vigour into it! You should be able to see your own reflection in all polished surfaces!' shouted Giles as he hovered over Melly, our nanny and general aide.

'Stop it!' I hissed. 'Melanie's not a pre-War housemaid. Get on with your work and stop shouting encouragement.'

'But it would be very rewarding for her,' barked Giles.

He always enjoyed the ritual at his prep school where, once a year, the whole school would take their bedding outside and, with two boys at the end of each blanket, shake it until powder puffs of grey dust filled the air. 'It was a symbol of the turning year,' he says. His interest in spring-cleaning was rekindled by his viewing of the film *The Remains of the Day*. He was deeply impressed by the mass cleaning sequences in which silver and surfaces were polished to a zealotic finish by an army of staff. Giles identified with Anthony Hopkins in his role as head butler and had hoped to introduce some of the rigours of the upkeep of a country house into our own little shelter.

'The hierarchy of servants, the complex system of privileges ... they appeal to people,' he expounded. 'The popularity of *Upstairs Downstairs* was no accident. There is a natural social order and deep in our psyche all Britons still occupy a rung on these social ladders . . .'

'I'm sure you're right,' I yawned. 'Why don't you write a new series, set in our cottage and called *Downstairs Downstairs*?'

Some days later I came upon an exemplary scene – Giles playing Lego with our daughter in front of a crackling fire as the rain poured off the thatch in a continuous veil, rather like the sudden artificial downpours of old black-and-white films. An ambitious construction, four storeys high was taking shape. I presumed it to be a house, but was swiftly corrected. It was a prison, complete with laundry, kitchen and sentries on a watch-tower.

My daughter explained that good prisoners were allowed some freedom to play and had windows in their cells but the really wicked ones were boxed in completely. She proudly lifted the roof to let me peep in to observe a dozen one-inch-high Lego people face downwards in this black hole. Their only crime? They had dropped litter in the exercise yard.

'Why can't you make farmyards or houses instead of prisons?' I asked Giles, who was chuckling with satisfaction.

'The punitive element seems to hold her attention longer than might a domestic scene,' he answered as he pretended to capture two escaped Lego convicts as they headed for the perimeter fence.

I had wondered why our daughter had developed an excessive reaction to litter. On a trip to the Botanical Gardens in Oxford she had become distressed by something small in the manicured flowerbeds under a witch hazel tree. Expecting to see the tiny corpse of a dying robin or small mammal, we clucked our way towards her, but could see nothing. 'Look, can't you see it? A cigarette end,' she cried in outrage.

'Litter always played a large part in my childhood,' Giles

told me. 'My parents always hated litter and Pip Wood was the very opposite of a young offender in his teenage years.' While his churlish contemporaries were emptying ashtrays and throwing cans of beer out of car windows, Pip Wood, or the Young Messiah, as Giles used to call him, roamed the byways near the local beauty spot, black dustbin sack in hand, picking up bushels of detritus.

'Somewhere along the line your family's policeman gene must have become over-dominant,' I complained. 'Nothing makes you happier than catching me in out in some petty crime like leaving a heater on – now you're training Freya to be a policewoman.'

But he insisted the petty policeman trait was not a genetic defect. 'It's because throughout my schooling I was constantly reminded that I was being trained to be a leader of men. As it turns out I am self-employed and have no men to lead so perhaps this meting out of just deserts to Lego people is just a harmless outlet for my thwarted leadership skills.'

One day I saw his face animated as he strode about the garden, pointing and waving at some grimy men who had turned up with a giant suction pipe. 'One of the few occasions I have to show leadership is when I inspect the cottage cesspit, to see if it needs emptying and then supervising the men when they turn up to do it,' he said happily.

With the end of Empire and the decline of the army there must be innumerable frustrated Englishmen whose instincts and training have prepared them to go out and rule vast tracts of Africa or give orders to hundreds of men. Yet we must learn to be more understanding of their plight – with no one to rule over but their families, what can the millions of leaders *manqués* do to improve their lot, short of adjudicating at vegetable and flower shows, refereeing football matches, becoming driving instructors or lecturing nannies and schoolgirls on the subject of litter?

DOWNWARD
MOBILITY

The publication of the first classless Honours List was of particular interest to my husband and me. Seven years ago we moved to a 'real' village with – apart from ourselves – 'real' people living in it. The village retains much of its feudal character, comprising thirteen households, whose denizens range in rank from serfs to noblemen, and even include a yeoman farmer.

In such a situation it is hard to believe that a classless society will ever come about. Indeed in my own household – a squat terraced cottage thrown up 150 years ago as shelter for workmen – there is a daily class struggle between my husband and myself. The other day he diagnosed our precise condition with relish.

'You're upwardly mobile and I'm downwardly!'

Yet Giles's attempts at social sinking are constantly thwarted as he meets with rebuttals at every turn. Once a year the entire village gathers together for the Fireworks Party given by the nobleman in the Old Rectory. The guests gravitate to the social milieu in which they feel most comfortable, as in a Gilbert & Sullivan opera. The middle classes circulate with glasses of mulled wine, Barbours and inane smiles, while the yocals, as they might be called, come dressed in paramilitary uniform and huddle round the bonfire drinking cans of lager. Meanwhile the upper classes, distinguished by their superior height, are in charge of the explosions. In this shadowy throng Giles can be seen moving between the groups trying to be all things to all men.

His ambition is that one day he will simultaneously gain the approval of both agricultural workers and squires, but in his conversational skirmishes he gets it wrong. He barks to the yocals in a strange modified accent about the absurd cost of the fireworks – 'You can't help feeling it's money that could have been better spent elsewhere,' he growls in a thick Wiltshire accent. 'Like on providing some local amenities.' Receiving no reaction, he retreats to the Barbours, and I overhear him saying to his hostess: 'What a marvellous display! Even better than last year.'

One summer's day after mulching his trees he walked to the pub in his boiler suit, intent on joining his fellow labourers on the land for gossip and relaxation but, as he made his way into the public bar, the cackle-raising anecdote in progress was cut short. Worse still, a hush descended on the company, which drained its tankards and filed out of the bar and into the sunshine. Ten years of private education had left its mark. Giles was 'them' to 'us'. Inverted snobbery had won. A different language and culture separates the public from the saloon bar.

Earlier excursions were more successful, when we had first come to the village and were an unknown quantity. Then Giles posed as a nerd and asked questions like, 'What's the pecking order round here?' Yet this backfired when a pub friend, the butler at the big house in the next village, saw Giles drinking champagne 'Upstairs' with his employer, a local grandee.

Despite these setbacks, he continues to try to throw off the yoke of the professional classes by chameleon-like behaviour, but is continually hoist by his own petard. Shortly after our arrival in the village, Giles was making his way across the fields further along the valley when he saw what was unmistakably a local swineherd walking towards him.

'Allo thar!' Giles barked ingratiatingly. 'New to these parts round 'ere. Is this quickest way back to village?'

The reply came back in clipped upper-class tones. 'If you tell me exactly which part of the village you are aiming for I will give you precise instructions.'

First impressions are lasting: this is one local grandee who has never invited us to drink champagne.

RIVALRY WITH
HIS FRIENDS
– HARRY

When is a friend not a friend? When he is a rival. You have
to occasionally keep your wits about you when mystified as
to why your husband seems to be either insidiously or openly
'baiting' his friends, and remember it's a simple matter of
rivalry.

Sometimes it's to do with the friend having more money.
Sometimes it's to do with his having less skill at the same
talent. Sometimes, and this is a shocking thing to say, you
may find one of your husband's friends flirting with you and
possibly even trying to go further just to see if you fancy him.
What horror to think your own husband might do the same
despicable thing! Don't give him the opportunity. As for old
schoolfriends, it's to do with having the same background
and history and then seeing who is doing the best with these
assets.

Giles has one friend from his schooldays, with whom
competition in later life has turned into what they both
laughingly describe as a 'decathlon'. Even a visit to an Indian
restaurant will turn into a competition, a trial of strength
between Giles and Harry to see which of them can endure
the hottest curry. Invariably, Harry wins because he orders

lobster phall, a curry too far for Giles who says his limit 'for medical reasons' is a vindaloo.

Every so often Harry turns up in England out of the blue. In 1989 he and his family left the country to live permanently in Kenya. Exchanging an indifferent lifestyle in south London for a lotus-eating exile in the sun, they timed their departure to coincide with some of the most demoralising years the country has ever undergone. Visits from this white settler have an unsettling effect on us as it seems blindingly obvious that hour by hour, day by day, his family's quality of life is better than ours is. Why on earth aren't we living in Kenya too?

As a former county runner, Harry still enjoys the competitive aspects of life. He usually adopts a hectoring and inquisitorial tone with his old best friend. 'Still doing odd jobs, Giles?' he asked last time we saw him.

'No,' Giles replied curtly. 'I'm a painter, a plantsman and a writer . . . in that order.'

Harry chuckled. 'It seems to me you're a chauffeur. All you've been doing this week is driving Mary up and down to London . . .'

Another seed of doubt was successfully sown. Giles sometimes refers to Harry as his 'worst man' as, while he waited for me to arrive at the altar, Harry, standing beside him, kept hissing, 'It's not too late to change your mind.'

Even after years of not seeing one another, Giles and Harry soon fall back into the familiar banter they developed as students. 'Don't you miss the seasons?' asked Giles unconvincingly, as we drove Harry from London to our cottage while the rain and wind buffeted the car.

Ignoring the question, Harry remarked on the number of four-wheel drive vehicles overtaking us. 'Why do people buy them in England?' he scoffed. 'This is the one country in the world where you don't need four-wheel drive!'

'They're *de rigueur* for the chattering classes,' Giles

explained. 'It's all to do with the extra height. Looking down on people is a national pastime.'

'And who are the chattering classes?' whined Harry.

'Anyone who collects, or even talks about collecting, edible fungi,' Giles enlightened him.

Arriving at the cottage, Harry knocked his head on a beam and cursed in Swahili. 'It's so cold in your cottage!' he shouted. 'Do you know I've been thinking about it since I've been back in England and I've realised that the only advantage this country has over Kenya is that you don't need to buy a refrigerator.'

A moment later we found him building a fire big enough to barbecue a Thompson's gazelle in our diminutive grate. Giles rushed forward. 'Hang on a minute, Harry. Don't forget it's a thatched cottage.'

'Don't be ridiculous; the thatch is wet,' said Harry. 'It rains every day in England.'

Harry went through to his bedroom, complaining, 'Oh no! I'd forgotten you have to unpack your own suitcase in this country.'

At breakfast the next morning, Harry piped up with: 'So what do you do for a good time in a tiny village in Wiltshire, with the winter approaching? This time tomorrow I'll be back in Africa,' he crowed, 'watching rhino and buffalo from a tree house. We spend literally hours up there with the children.'

'I'm not surprised, you're probably too scared to come down,' grumbled Giles. 'Before you go back to your fool's paradise, let's have a traditional English breakfast. Now that's something you can't get in Kenya.'

True to the tradition of their twenty-year friendship, Giles's voice was soon heard from the kitchen. 'Oh dear, Harry, your egg's broken. What a pity because mine's just right . . .'

'Nothing changes,' grinned Harry.

PEER
PRESSURE

'Kate's on the telephone,' I screamed down the staircase. 'She says can she bring a friend to lunch.'

Giles burst through the kitchen door in a cloud of steam. 'No, she certainly can't,' he snapped. 'We haven't got enough food or drink and the cottage is too small.' He glared up at me, then said, 'Ask her if it's a male friend or a female.'

'Male,' came Kate's reply.

'Well, we can hardly say no,' hissed Giles. 'But he'll have to sit quietly in a corner. I don't want to be threatened in my own cottage. Is he a small man? That might be all right.'

I thrust the telephone at him. 'Of course you can bring him,' said Giles, changing personality and exuding charm. 'Who is it anyway? Do I know him?'

'What's his name?' I asked when Giles had hung up. He told me.

'Well,' I informed him, 'not only is he not a small man, he's a roughly six-foot-three-inched stately home owner.'

'What a nightmare,' said Giles. 'There's nothing worse than a steaming cottage on a wet Sunday afternoon in January. We can't even see out of the windows because of

64

the condensation. For someone who normally lives in a stately home, it'll be like going inside a kettle.'

Giles's sister was on a skiing holiday so her two dogs were staying with us. The floors were covered with Beast of Dartmoor-style footprints. 'And why does she have to bring him on the one day when I'm serving the most disgusting lunch I've cooked in years?'

One of Giles's chief attractions was his culinary expertise, but for some reason – 'probably to annoy myself' as he says – our cottage fare has recently been rather hit and miss. 'It's a disaster,' he said, pushing a ladle of pigeon casserole towards my face. 'All because you bought frozen pigeon breasts. You should have gone to the shoe-heel bar and asked for some leather offcuts. They would have been cheaper and the taste would have been identical.'

It was too late to change the menu. Giles decided to Magimix the pigeon breasts to make their presence less offensive. The result was a brown gruel worthy of a Victorian workhouse kitchen.

When Kate arrived, her companion had to stoop down low to avoid hitting his head on the door jamb as he came in. Giles had already prepared his opening gambit.

'Welcome to our humble abode. I hope you will share a simple meal with us. I understand you're a lord?'

'Certainly not,' said our guest. 'Lords are two a penny. I'm a peer of the realm.' This served to break the ice and Giles asked him to 'take a pew'.

'Do you enjoy eating game?' Giles enquired.

'Very much,' replied Lord X. 'But I tend to steer clear of vermin – squirrel, rabbit and pigeon for example.' We laughed merrily. After we had toyed with the gruel, and more or less concentrated on the wine, Giles whipped away the leathern mixture and poured it into the dogs' bowl in one swift action. 'Is anyone still hungry?' he enquired.

'Would you like a fried egg with your coffee, or perhaps a cup of tea? We do a nice Earl Grey!'

'Do I detect an undercurrent of republicanism in this house?' asked the earl, good-naturedly.

'Not at all,' insisted Giles. 'A mere accident of birth is all that separates us. A paternalistic oligarchy is just what the country needs as we approach the millennium.'

Later Giles explained to me that he had been nursing a chip on his shoulder with regard to the aristocracy ever since he had attended the wedding of the Marquess of W and realised that not only the groom but most of the fellow male guests seemed to be 'a good foot taller than me'. (Giles is five foot ten.)

'Harry said it was because they had lived on a diet of fillet steak since birth and since I was reared on chicken – and pigeon and other vermin, it was hardly surprising.'

But Lord X had the last laugh. As he was leaving, Giles ventured, 'This is probably the first time you have been into a cottage . . .'

'No, I often go into cottages,' replied Lord X. 'But usually only to evict tenants.'

DRIVING
YOU MAD

Cyril was addressing the Cheltenham Literary Festival and had asked us to join him for dinner. As we set off I noticed that our Lada Riva estate car was juddering. 'What's happening?' I panicked.

'Just testing the brakes,' said Giles. 'There may be an intermittent fault. They probably don't have to use brakes very often in Russia.'

I should have learned from experience not to rise to this particular bait. Just as he never presents a chicken without saying, 'It may not be cooked through,' Giles's pointless speculation about the brakes form a predictable part of every car journey.

'Why not have them checked in a garage, then?' I always ask.

'No, it's all right,' he sighs. 'I think they're fine.' It is a script from which we rarely deviate.

The trouble is that, despite having had forty lessons, I still cannot drive and am never sure whether or not to be anxious when being driven by others. 'Look, I'm in charge. Just sit back and let me do the driving,' says Giles. But moments later I point out a red light towards which we are hurtling.

'Just as well you spotted that,' he says, braking abruptly. 'We make a good team.'

'I don't want to be part of a driving team!' I cry. 'Does that mean you would have gone through that light?'

'I probably would have seen it eventually, but two heads are better than one.'

Am I to sit on the edge of my seat giving a running commentary on changing road conditions, or can I relax with a magazine with total confidence in my driver? It seems neither is the case.

Cars are something of a metaphor for marriage, being a concentrated version of it, and when boxed in together all one's strengths and weaknesses are brought into sharp focus. One friend, Andrew, blames his marriage break-up partly on driving: 'Certainly some of the worst moments of my marriage happened in the car,' he remembers. I told him that on the few occasions when I had been driven by him I had found his habit of spurting fairly annoying. Andrew denied the spurting was his fault, saying that 'all cheap automatic cars do that'.

Both Giles and I find it impossible to perform the twin tasks of concentrating on road signs and driving at the mandatory racetrack speeds round the one-way systems of modern British cities. There can be no room for mistakes as you search for the correct lane with young offenders in fast cars surging all around you. When we got to Cheltenham, the only option was to go round and round the inner ring road, both shouting 'Which way now?' I was to blame, of course; as the non-driver I was the chief navigator, but we both shouted 'It's not my fault!' as the cars closed in around us. As we lapped the inner ring for the third time, we chanced upon our destination.

It was Cyril's seventh wedding anniversary and at dinner his wife Ursula revealed to us that the only time she had ever seen Cyril deliriously happy, apart from at the birth of their children, was when she got directions wrong on car journeys and he could catch her out as incompetent.

Trying to leave Cheltenham, we drove round its suburbs for hours following diversion signs for Cirencester, but kept ending up in the same place. There was a sign for Oxford and in fear for our sanity, we took it. Neither of us felt intelligent enough to pull into a lay-by and try to work out a sensible alternative route but we did know the way home from Oxford. We chose to head for there. 'Driving is so much easier than thinking,' said Giles. I agreed, even though the round trip via Oxford added forty minutes to the journey.

The following day I told Andrew on the telephone about how tense these nightmare drives were making me feel. He listened carefully then gave the following piece of advice. 'X and Y have only just divorced after thirty years of marriage,' he told me, referring to two friends of his I hardly know. 'Through all that time they kept their marriage together by adhering to one simple rule. They never went on a long car journey in the same car.'

LOOKING
FOR
THINGS

Looking at some old photographs one morning I found one
of myself wearing a beautiful Irish scarf that I had quite
forgotten about. This antique textile had been given to me
by a great-aunt and was woven from the finest pastel-
coloured linens. It was big enough to double as a shawl and
one of the loveliest clothes I have ever owned. Where is it
now? I fumed, as it sank in that I had not seen it for years.

Later that same morning I realised that Giles was looking
for his wallet again, and had been for some time. Within
seconds of my starting to look, I had found it. I thrust it at
him aggressively.

'Ah! There it was,' he crowed. 'I did say I knew I hadn't
lost it. You see,' he went on. 'We're living in a dark cottage
where most of the surfaces are black – all these tables are
black, the piano is black – so it shouldn't be surprising that
someone should have difficulty in finding a black wallet,
should it?'

'No,' I snapped, 'but it *is* surprising that a person who
can't find his wallet in a dark cottage *every single morning*, and
spends an hour looking for it *every single morning*, doesn't get
into the habit of leaving it in a set place every night when he

comes in. It *is* surprising that you are prepared to lose the equivalent of one working day per week blundering around looking for your wallet.'

'Dear, dear,' Giles tutted. 'That sounds very like someone who's angry with herself. Could you possibly be projecting because you've lost your Irish scarf and you didn't even realise it until you saw some old photographs?'

How could it ever have been the case that, as students, we used to think it was funny or somehow cool to lose things? Giles and his Fulham flatmates used to bristle with pride when they forgot which street they had parked their car in. Once they toured the neighbourhood in a taxi looking for it, drawling 'Now, can we go down that street again? I forgot to look.' It was an extravagant gesture but worth it for the kudos it brought in from fellow art students. And it was *de rigueur* to laugh in warm approval when friends announced that they had left something on the roof of their car while they unlocked the door, then driven off with whatever it was still on the roof, losing it somewhere along the journey. You know – it was cool, because it proved you were unmaterialistic about possessions.

One friend who spent hours each day looking for her house keys was given a bleeping key-ring by her mother. You whistled into the chaos and the key-ring bleeped back. But my friend never replaced the batteries when they ran down. Being unable to find her keys was a statement of identity. It showed that she was a free, artistic spirit and unbourgeois.

'And do you remember being "out of it"?' Giles reminisced. 'Those were the days when we thought it was hilarious to have no idea where we were, what we were in the middle of doing or what time of day it was.'

At what age does being 'out of it' cease to be cool and start becoming a sign of encroaching senile dementia? If every teenager becomes the thing he most despises, I imagine it will not be long now before Giles and I start hanging keys up on hooks, finding a place for everything and putting everything in its place, getting our stuff ready the night before we go to London – why, even rehearsing packing, like Giles's late father.

'It's not that you've got encroaching dementia,' said a doctor friend. 'It's just that you're beginning to realise why older people spend so much time putting things back in their places, writing things down in diaries and confirming things in writing. Experience has taught them what happens if they don't.'

At least I can look forward to one advancement of the technological age – the inevitable introduction of bleeping electronic tags which can be affixed to all possessions. What a time-saver they will be for members of the post-cool pre-dementia generation.

THE
OLD SCHOOL
NEWSLETTER

'I wonder what became of Le Quesne?' said Giles. He was reading his Old Salopian newsletter at the breakfast table we had set up in the garden.

'I expect he's something in the City, earning a hundred K and buying his wife a new dress occasionally,' I replied. 'Most of your contemporaries will be on six figures by now. Some may even have retired.'

'Well I bet he hasn't got four nest-boxes full of young birds in his back garden. Not to mention a bumble-bee colony,' Giles chuckled. 'That's what I call success! Good God, look at the obituaries . . . G has died. He was only my age. He was always swotting for his exams, now he's probably died from over-work and stress. Poor blighter.'

'Well,' I pulled a 'realistic' face, 'don't forget you'll be forty in a few years. You can expect your school contemporaries to be burnt out by now or having their first heart attacks.'

'Yes,' agreed Giles enthusiastically. 'It's just as well I never went into advertising. I was always told I should. If I had done I would definitely have burnt out by now.'

'Still,' I mused. 'You would have enjoyed some financial rewards along the way . . .'

'Don't forget the fable of the tortoise and the hare.' He wagged his finger.

'What about it?'

'Well, I'm the tortoise,' he nodded.

'I think the tortoise actually entered the race didn't it?'

He ignored this remark. 'I expect G took his work too seriously,' he said. 'I think I've got the balance between work and leisure about right.'

Suddenly I noticed a chubby little bird sitting on one of the bird-boxes chirping at the top of its voice.

'Why is that bird not going into the box?' I asked. 'Is it too big for the hole or something? What type of bird is it?'

'Think, Mary, think! I've told you a hundred times before.'

'Thrush, lapwing, swallow . . . no – starling.'

'Wrong on all four counts,' said Giles. 'It's a golden eagle.'

He strode contemptuously off down the garden to dead-head his roses.

'Hang on.' I followed him. 'You haven't answered your Old Salopian questionnaire. Shall I fill it in for you? Here's a box for you to list your charitable works.'

'How absurd! Put "generous street contributions to Greenpeace and Friends of the Earth".'

'What about "New Year's Honours or Titles"?'

'My services to wildlife conservation haven't been officially recognised yet,' he answered. 'Hey, come and look at this. Something's happened to my bee colony . . . Something very big and powerful has dug it out. There are dead bees everywhere! You don't suppose it's a badger?'

We stared in dismay at the genocidal scene. 'Shall I call the council?' I suggested. 'We don't want the garden to be full of swarming bees.'

'I'm pretty sure this is Brock's work. Look at the mess he's made,' complained Giles.

While he went in search of village elders for a second opinion on the 'Beast of Wiltshire' I saw for myself what looked like a mortar blast in the middle of the lawn. This was no stray dog's work.

Soon a procession of elders were in the garden, giving their opinions. 'I'm not being funny or anything . . . but that's badger all right,' came the message. 'They're after the honey.'

'You see the bees don't sting them because their skins are four feet thick,' vouchsafed another.

'Surely four inches thick . . .' I suggested.

'You know what this means,' said Giles portentously. 'It means our garden is so successful as a wildlife sanctuary that larger mammals up the food chain are starting to colonise. Who knows where it'll end. Wild boars may introduce themselves next. I'm a victim of my own success. What's the point of me turning the field back to herb-rich meadow to attract bees if badgers are then going to commit bee genocide?' He began to rant. 'It makes a nonsense of animal rights if the animals themselves are going to be complete bastards. We're going to have to get rid of this badger.'

The last question for the school register was a box for occupation. 'What shall I put, Mary? Ecologist, Grounds-man, Chauffeur, Artist or Ornithologist?'

'How about Pest Controller?' I suggested.

PARTNERS IN
TIME-WASTING

'I've just ordered the bronze turkey and I've arranged to collect it on the Friday before Christmas Eve,' said Giles as he struck the word 'turkey' off a long list headed 'Christmas Countdown'.

'Where is this organic meat farm?' I asked.

'Shrivenham . . . ?' he replied carelessly. 'I'm not sure. Somewhere between Swindon and Oxford, I think.'

'Well, why didn't you have it delivered?' I groaned. 'The traffic will be bumper to bumper and it will take you the whole day to get there and back.'

'Aha! Because I'm saving six pounds by picking it up myself,' he lectured. 'Now you can't say six pounds isn't worth saving because six pounds equals two chickens.'

The 'chicken' is a basic unit of currency to Giles and he counts it as being roughly equivalent to three pounds in money.

'But you'll spend at least six pounds in petrol collecting it!' I raged. 'Not to mention wasting a whole day which you could have spent finishing a painting which could bring in hundreds of chickens. Just ring them back and tell them to deliver it.'

'I'm sorry, Mary. My mind's made up.'

'Don't call me Mary!' I screamed.

One of the main causes of marital breakdown is supposed to be a failure to communicate and I was fortunate that Giles quickly decided to admit to us both the real reason for this act of Pyrrhic budgeting. 'Actually,' he confessed, 'I was rather looking forward to exploring that part of the country and seeing Wayland's Smithy and Uffington Castle.' Realising in a flash that we had an old friend near Uffington Castle whom it might be rather festive to see on that day, I quickly back-pedalled. 'Perhaps you're right.' I said. 'I'll come with you.'

The chicken as a basic unit of currency.

It seems we can both find plenty of time to do the things we enjoy but there is no time available for the duller and more difficult duties. For months Giles has been 'too busy' to buy a new pair of glasses. This despite complaining of seeing Christmas lights in our local high street all the year round as car headlights are refracted in the ice rinks that were once his lenses. But a nagging headache meant he could delay it no longer. 'I've found a window of opportunity to visit the optician,' he announced. 'My prescription may need to be changed.' Knowing that with new lenses alone starting at thirty chickens he might go for the cheapest frames in another act of Pyrrhic budgeting, I asked to go with him.

'In and out,' he insisted before we entered the shop.

'Twenty minutes at the most,' I reassured him.

'It's always difficult to confront your own appearance,' he had confessed as we entered the shop. In the event he had forgotten how much he enjoyed the sight test and he exchanged views with the optician about the latest developments in laser surgery for myopia. Then came the striking of attitudes – modelling different frames in front of a mirror – but the best was yet to come. Haine & Smith have introduced a videotape and TV screen system enabling customers to see themselves as others see them.

'Can we just run through it again?' said a fascinated Giles to the dapper assistant as they watched the sixty-second film of the shortlisted three frames time and again.

'No problem,' he said with the patience of a saint.

We eventually chose a pair with virtually invisible frames and whose lenses mimicked the shape of the eyes and were only millimetres larger. 'Are you sure they're not too KGB agent?' asked Giles. The assistant assured him that they were 'the latest style from the Continent' and that clinched it.

One and a half hours after entering we left the opticians to go to Cots & Tots to exchange a toy. There we found a notice reading 'Back in five minutes' – surely the most annoying four words in the English language.

'Five minutes!' I expostulated. 'We can't possibly waste that amount of time.' We stood for at least five marvelling at the vulgarity of a festive window display nearby. Then a polite voice interrupted our reveries.

'Can I ask for a few minutes of your time, sir and madam? We're just conducting some market research and would like to get your answers to a few questions.'

'I'm very sorry. We're in a bit of a hurry,' we replied in unison as we quickened our steps towards Waitrose.

TRAVEL
FEVER

'May I make a suggestion without you flying off the handle?' asked Giles.

He had come upon me in our bedroom. I was standing over a suitcase and, with my eyes shut and my lips mouthing silently, I was clearly going through a mental check-list.

'What?' I said shortly.

'Don't take anything that you're not going to need.'

'Giles!' I screamed.

'There's no need to behave badly in front of the children,' he said in a calm and steady voice. 'If I'm going to have to carry four people's luggage then I want you to pare things down to the absolute essentials – there's no need to take that *Just William* tape, for example.'

'But it's as light as a feather. And in any case we'll get a trolley at Heathrow.'

'It all adds up. I think what's most important is that we get off now rather than hanging about the house maundling.'

'Fine,' I said. 'So we'll get off without the things that we need, then? *Without* the baby's milk? *Without* Freya's nightdress? *Without* the plane tickets? *Without* the book I'm going to read while I'm there and *without* my wallet?'

'No, you can get those. All I am saying is that I want to get off in very good time so that there's no panic if we run into traffic or there is any unexpected delay. I'm thinking ahead, you see. So quickly, be quick. Quick!'

Soon the cottage seemed tinier than ever as a delinquent pile of luggage blocked access through the dining-room. This was the pared-down version of absolute essentials needed for a routine five-day visit to my family home in Northern Ireland. Any mother would have had difficulty reducing the volume with pushchair, clip-on high chair, bottle-warmer, nappies and snuggle suits to be loaded before we even started on wellington boots.

Giles's own luggage, by contrast, stood little larger than a briefcase. 'I think you'll agree I've been very efficient with my own packing,' he said.

'I don't know if I do agree,' I said. 'It looks to me as if you've done Pyrrhic packing again. It's all very well travelling light but it's a bit short-sighted to travel so light that you exclude yourself from all activities on arrival through having nothing to wear and none of the equipment you need. Have you packed a jacket for example?'

'Why would I need a jacket in Northern Ireland?'

Halfway to Heathrow, Giles suddenly spat his medicated lozenge into a tissue. 'You did turn off the blow-fire didn't you? I mean you would have heard it whirring, wouldn't you? Well, did you?'

'Did you?' I replied. 'Why should I hear it any more than you?'

After a few moments of torturing him I said, 'Well, thank goodness Mrs Pankhurst is going in to clean this afternoon, so she'll be able to turn it off . . . Oh no, I've just realised. You haven't left your key in the back door, have you?'

'That's right,' Giles nodded. 'To keep Bill Burglar out. What's wrong with that?'

'Did it not occur to you that Mrs Pankhurst won't be able to turn her key in the lock, if there's one already in it?'

Giles sighed heavily. 'I think we'd better not go anywhere again. It's too stressful. We must be middle-aged. It's taking too much out of us.'

By the time we had reached Heathrow he had almost finished his second packet of Tunes. 'We must buy some more,' he exclaimed. 'I'm very blocked up. Hang on, how many packets of Tunes am I allowed in one day? I don't want to exceed the maximum dose.'

'You are becoming middle-aged. Do you think Ranulph Fiennes carries on like this every time he sets out on a journey?' I chided.

Despite being seasoned travellers we have found, since we had the children, that there is always an atmosphere of panic about our party, as though we had strayed off the set of *Carry On Travelling*. Having left the car in the Pink Elephant Car Park, we found that for once we had time to spare before our flight and could actually 'relax' in the Departure Lounge. 'I think I deserve coffee and a croissant now,' said Giles.

But even now there was something bothering him. The coffee cups were too wide. 'She's given us coffee soup. It's going to take us forty-five minutes just to drink all this up. I'm going to complain.' But we were summoned to our seats and left the bowls of coffee undrunk. Once in the air, Giles was soon complaining again. 'If only I hadn't bought that coffee and croissant. No one told us there would be a three-course meal on the plane.'

'No one's forcing you to eat it,' I said.

But when we arrived at my mother's house in County Antrim, she ushered us straight in to a homely lunch of chicken soup and soda bread. 'You must be starving, Giles!' she said.

'Well, not really . . .' Giles began, but no one was interested in the fact that he had eaten two packets of Tunes, a croissant, two beef sandwiches, four salmon sandwiches, four fingers of chocolate and four cups of coffee.

'Will you have some more, Giles?' my mother asked him after his second helping.

'No thanks, I'd better have a rest if you don't mind. I'm feeling a bit odd.'

'So strange for a young man to need a rest,' said my mother.

HE'S
ALWAYS
RIGHT

'Look. I don't believe it! There's another one,' said Giles.

'Another what?' I asked.

'Another white plastic bag caught in a tree. Is it a tradition here in Northern Ireland to have bags in the trees?'

I ignored his question. 'Just concentrate on the road and stop looking out for eyesores.'

The plastic bags were starting to thin out as we left the town behind in our sleek blue hire car and soon the spectacular Antrim Coast Road opened up before us. We were heading for Glenarrif, the most beautiful of Antrim's nine glens and the sombre slow movement of Bruckner's Fifth accompanied us as the winter sunshine spot-lit the majestic headlands.

Before the Troubles there were three grand hotels in my local town, each packed to the brim with holiday-makers as the Antrim Coast Road was considered to be the second most beautiful in Europe after the Corniche. It was still as beautiful now and our only troubles were self-inflicted. Our driver was writhing in his seat like an escapologist.

'Are you having a fit or something?' I enquired.

'No,' said Giles, 'but I've just spotted a drawer marked "Coins" and I'm transferring my money from my pockets.'

'Don't be ridiculous,' I shrieked, as the car wandered to the wrong side of the road. 'You'll just forget the money is there when you hand the car back. It's probably a well-known ruse in the car hire world to actually install coin drawers to fleece people.'

'Well,' said Giles airily. 'I'll bet you the contents of the drawer that I don't forget it.'

'Look, Daddy!' interjected Freya. 'A waterfall.'

In England there would be signs saying 'To the Waterfall', a car-park and an award-winning interpretation centre-cum-restaurant, but here in Ireland we were able to interpret it for ourselves. I stayed in the car with the baby while Giles and Freya struck out towards the gushing torrent. I could see through the windscreen the little rivulets at the top joining together at the middle in a stream which was whipped up again by the gale force winds in a Turnerian vortex.

Half an hour later three heads loomed up at the hire car window, one of which was a skull. 'Yuck!' I screamed. 'Why have you picked that up?'

'Because I'm an artist and I'm going to draw it,' said Giles, loading the feral goat's skull into the boot.

Back home I helped him to smuggle a cup of bleach and an old bucket from my mother's kitchen with which to clean the skull. 'Would your mother be interested in seeing it?' Giles grinned.

'No, I shouldn't think she'll see the point of it. After all, she can scarcely see the point of you at the moment since you broke the lock on the bathroom door by wrenching it when it had worked quite well as it was for thirty years.'

Back in Wiltshire, Giles was still wringing his hands about the latest mishap. As I had foretold he had forgotten to collect his loose change from the coin drawer. 'You were right,' said Giles. 'Now that man who hired me the car will be having scampi in the basket at my expense.'

'Well cheer up. I'll waive my winnings,' I said kindly.

'And at least the goat's skull was free,' said Giles. 'That reminds me. Freya!' He called our daughter into the bathroom and taking the goat's skull in one hand and an old suede brush in the other, he began to clean the caprine molars. 'Look, Freya, this is how hard I want you to brush. Really get into those cracks between your teeth like this. Up and down!' For the first time ever Freya seemed to comprehend the full importance of dental hygiene.

'Well, blow me down,' I said magnanimously. 'You were right too. The goat skull was worth bringing home after all.'

CLUTTER

'Do you save empty boxes and spare parts to unknown things?' read Giles aloud.

'Yes,' I said. 'Of course I do. Why?'

'You know I had no idea how brilliant *Reader's Digest* is,' he enthused. 'It's literally full of wisdom. This article explains in just two pages exactly why living in our cottage is so difficult. It's called "Unclutter your life". Listen to this. "Have you squirrelled away pieces of timber from an unfinished project?" Yes! "Is your garage filled with derelict garden furniture . . . ?" '

'Well we don't have a garage,' I drawled. 'In our case it's the furniture in the house which is derelict.'

'It says we must make an appointment with ourselves to unclutter our lives,' Giles read on. ' "The pay-off may include a greater sense of freedom." '

'Surely that's never been a problem for you?' I remarked. 'You've got too much freedom already.'

'Please try to be less like Hilda Ogden,' he groaned. 'Now let's each take a room. In the first sweep we'll get rid of anything that is obvious junk. Then after lunch I will apply the test.'

Freya was thrilled at the idea of a test. 'What is the test, Daddy?' she asked eagerly.

' "Items displayed in the house should have a valid reason for being there",' he read. ' "If the antique clock in the hall no longer works, for instance, then it has lost its function and it must go." '

'Does the same apply if your husband doesn't work?' I asked. 'Wouldn't it be a better use of your Bank Holiday weekend for you to finish that commission and thereby introduce new money into the household rather than lose money by throwing things out?'

'Aha!' he cried. 'That's where you're wrong. It says here that clutter can in fact cost you money because you end up buying things you already have but you just can't see them because of the clutter.'

'Like the clothes pegs we buy every week,' chipped in Freya.

'Exactly! Well done, Freya. Okay then. As it's raining we will each do a room. Go to it. Out! Out! Out!' he cried, raising his arms like a weight-lifter to mimic the actions of stuff being loaded on to a bonfire in our field.

I was drained of my usual fighting spirit due to going down with something caught from a coughing co-passenger on the train from London. The thought of imminent hospitalisation reminded me of how happy I always am in hospital when surrounded only by a limited number of my own possessions with all their mentally draining reverbera-tions. 'Go ahead,' I croaked weakly. 'As long as you agree to put everything into the attic as a staging post to being thrown out.' In my bedroom I put in my earplugs as the crashing and banging began.

Time went by and I emerged from my room to find the cottage looking spartan. I had to admit the effect was relaxing. 'Once I had begun, it was only really a matter of common sense,' said Giles. 'Take the larder for example.

There is no need for us to have ten jugs. There would never be an occasion when we were going to use ten jugs of milk at once so I've put eight of them in the attic.'

'The reason we have ten is because we put flowers in them, not milk.'

'Well why on earth couldn't you have said that instead of lying in bed with earplugs in? And the other giant step forward I've made is to put all the clothes I haven't seen you wearing for more than six months into the attic.'

'Thanks a lot. The reason you haven't seen me wearing them is because it hasn't been summer for the last six months.'

Giles's face fell. 'Well at least we can see our way clear now to thinking ahead.'

'Yes,' I agreed. 'And I'm thinking ahead very clearly to next month when Cyril moves to Aldeburgh. Remember last time he moved house he left thousands of pounds worth of stuff behind because he was so impatient and disorganised? Well this time we can go along and stock up on all sorts of things like chairs, tables, books, records . . . there's plenty of room for them now . . .'

Giles went into the garden and began to scream.

IT'S
NOT
FAIR

'Gi-yles . . .' I called from an upstairs window, four feet above the ground. 'I haven't actually had one moment's relaxation today and it's seven o'clock. Can you tell me how much longer you're going to need before you're finished in the garden?'

'A lifetime!' shouted Giles from behind a hedge.

'What do you mean?' I groaned.

'Exactly that,' he answered cheerfully. 'A garden is never finished. It's a living, constantly evolving thing. All right then,' he conceded, 'let me just move these three shrubs to their final positions and then I'll come in.'

'I know gardening is your hobby,' I said, 'but why can't you plant the things in their final positions in the first place, instead of having to keep moving them?'

'You're not a gardener, you wouldn't understand,' said Giles. 'Anyway, it's not a hobby. Maintaining and developing the garden will add value to the property as a whole.'

'But we're not selling!'

'Stop quarrelling, Mummy and Daddy,' said Freya. 'Let Daddy do what he wants. It's his day.'

'But it's not fair!' I spluttered.

Though Freya's timely intervention brought the argument to a close it was not the first nor the last time that day that a bitter voice would be heard crying out somewhere in the cottage: 'It's not fair!' Indeed, on any given day we can be assured that at least one member of the family will be taking up the refrain at regular intervals.

Moving shrubs.

From our first burst balloon to the final undertaker's bill our lives are full of injustice and unfairness. If life is unfair in general, family life is unfair in particular and, unlike in industrial relations, there is no arbitration and conciliation service to hand.

Freya is getting to the age where she and virtually all of her contemporaries talk about whether or not things are fair most of the time. They are all obsessed with one little girl called Emily whose birthday is on Christmas Day and whose mother has succumbed to pressure and now gives her an official birthday in June, like the Queen, as well as her real birthday.

That evening, Freya thought it was deeply unfair when I

brought the crying baby downstairs during something unmissable on television. 'It's not fair. I want to come down too!'

'But it's not fair on me if I miss the programme!' I riposted.

And that morning it had been Giles's birthday, yet two of the cards from two favourite people which had been posted failed to arrive on time. In their place came a letter guaranteed to wipe the smile off his face. Reading it aloud, his face became so contorted with incredulity that Freya felt compelled to sit on his knee.

Thank you for your communication in connection with the penalty notice. It is not the policy of Westminster City Council to withdraw any tickets incurred because the initial payment was inserted into the wrong meter. While this rule may appear harsh in your particular case, please remember that it is the motorist's responsibility to observe the parking regulations correctly.

I regret I am unable to cancel the penalty charge notice and accordingly I shall be pleased to receive your remittance of £20 in settlement.

'Harsh indeed! Judge Jefferies would have shown more leniency. When I think of all the pound coins I've poured into those meters and in one frenetic moment rushing into a hospital to visit someone, I make a tiny error of judgement. It's just not fair,' moaned Giles.

'Well,' I said in schoolmistress tones. 'It may not be fair but perhaps it will come as a salutary experience. It may sharpen up your wits so that next time you go to London you don't make the same mistake again.'

'Right,' said Giles, making out the penalty cheque there

and then. 'Sadly it's your birthday next month and all I can say is there goes your present.'

'What do you mean?'

'Well this was the twenty pounds that I had set aside to buy your present. Now I won't be able to get you one.'

'Now that really isn't fair!' I protested.

'Stop quarrelling and open your presents, Daddy,' said Freya impatiently.

'Fair enough!' said Giles.

RIVALRY
WITH HIS MATES
– GERRY

As households go ours is caught in something of a technological time warp. We have neither microwave nor com-
puter games, colour TV set or compact disc player. We still
collect LPs and our Lada Riva estate car is apparently built on
obsolete technology. Our deprivation is partly to do with
affectation and partly to do with poverty, though the lack of
a colour television set is deliberate since both of us sit like
rabbits in headlights whenever we have access to one, and we
know we could watch the rest of our lives away.

The contrast between our lifestyle and that of our best
friends, the Farrells, came up when we stayed with them
recently.

'Dad! Freya hasn't got a video,' cried their son Fred in
tones of utter disbelief.

'What's more, they haven't even got a telly!' laughed
Gerry, as he lay back on a sofa surfing through the satellite
channels with the remote control switch. 'The Woods are an
underprivileged family – repeat after me.'

'Underprivileged,' echoed Fred in his quiet voice.

Later Giles fought back. 'Some day, Gerry, your body will
just implode from inactivity and junk food. All that will be

left of you will be a pool of Diet Coke with a remote control switch and a pair of glasses lying in it.'

This sort of banter is typical when we go to stay with our chums in Balham. 'Ring the Farrells and tell them we've arrived in London,' says Giles as we sweep off the M4 flyover. 'So it'll be another hour before we get to them.' We have an ongoing competition about which of our lifestyles is preferable – the urban or the rural. While we live in a tiny cottage in a lovely landscape, they live in a huge and beautiful house in a frightening area of London where their car is broken into at least once a month.

Going to stay at Fortress Farrell, as we call it, is always a treat because everything is so clean and new and there are televisions in every room. Fred Farrell's playroom is like a corner of Hamley's, and Jo Farrell's bathroom is like the Clinique counter at Harrods.

'I bet Freya can't count to a hundred in three different languages,' said Gerry, unwrapping a trilingual speaking calculator for his son. Gerry also has an aquarium and Freya is fascinated by his collection of genetically engineered Japanese fish which look as though they have been crossed with nasturtiums. A discarded bass guitar bears testimony to Gerry's short attention span. He has a fast turnover in hobbies – this week bonsai trees, next vintage cars.

Part of the joy in staying in their Balham pleasuredrome is the sheer luxury of it all: comfy sofas, thick carpets, piping hot water and all the latest consumer goods. The Farrells used to come to stay with us, but we're sufficiently close friends not to have taken offence when Gerry stated that the cottage was too uncomfortable for him and the conditions too primitive. The last time they came Giles proudly showed Gerry his plantation of native deciduous trees which he spends hundreds of man-hours per year mulching and staking in a desperate struggle against the Westerlies. 'Gilo! These trees have actually shrunk since the last time I saw them!'

laughed Gerry. Giles looked despondent. 'Come on, man,' Gerry urged him. 'Admit it – you're fighting a losing battle, you're miserable in the country. Come back to London.'

Back in Balham we took the children to the Common and a rapturous twenty-month-old Posy tottered like a clock-work toy towards the lake, scattering pitbull terriers and rottweilers in her wake. 'This is the first time she's run,' I gasped, as we ran after her. 'That's because she's never been on level ground before,' said Gerry. 'Why not move back to London where you've got playing fields to run on instead of horrid cow-patty turf?'

Soon it was. Saturday night. Giles and Gerry were preparing to go 'up West'.

'How do I look, Mary?' asked Giles.

'Really repulsive.'

'Good,' nodded Giles. 'That's the whole idea. When I get to the West End I want to merge into the crowd. I don't want to draw attention to myself by being too smartly dressed.'

Off they went, bound for the wretched fayre of cheese-burger and fries 'twice', followed by a viewing of a new space shocker, *Species*. This has all the ingredients for a toxic lads' night out of a type impossible to achieve in the country.

'How was it?' Jo and I asked on their return.

'Brilliant,' came their reply. 'I haven't had such a good time for years,' said Giles.

'Really? For as long as that?' I mused.

But Giles looked queasy on Sunday morning and couldn't face the full English breakfast prepared by Jo. He confessed that after seeing *Species* he and Gerry were so hungry that they went to Chinatown for a second meal. Now he imagined he was suffering from monosodium glutamate poisoning.

'Don't worry, we're going to the zoo,' said Gerry.

'You may be,' said Giles. 'I'm off to Kew Gardens.'

'In the Farrell household,' said Gerry sternly. 'We put our children first.'

We were not the only citizens to think of going to London Zoo that weekend. Humans outnumbered animals ten to one. 'Look, only minutes to go before the penguins' feeding time,' said Gerry cheerfully.

'It's amazing how you think there's anything natural about the zoo when you live in London,' Giles remarked. 'I feel exactly how that lion is looking. In fact I've never seen such a miserable-looking bunch of animals. Find me a stone, Gerry. I want to see if that penguin's dead or alive. It's been standing there motionless for ten minutes.'

'I've never seen Giles like this before,' said Jo. 'What on earth's wrong with him?'

'It's quite simple, Jo — it's past his feeding time. Let's go to the canteen before he throws himself into the lions' den.'

'Oh, I do love staying with the Farrells in London,' said Giles when he had restored his blood sugar levels. 'Can we do it every weekend?'

'No,' said Jo and Gerry in unison.

SECRETS

'What's the difference between the Famous Five and the Secret Seven?' I asked Freya patronisingly.

'Well,' she pondered, 'the Secret Seven are gooder than the Famous Five because they want to do good things in secret just like the Brownies or Pixies.'

For our little girl, secrets in general are synonymous only with happiness and excitement and good deeds. Fairies really do exist – only grown-ups don't know it. Caskets of treasure are hidden all over the place and midnight feasts are the very highlights of her life.

Secrets for her grown-up mother still hold their charms. As they trickle in throughout the week I spend many happy hours gasping 'No!' into the telephone. What pleasure they give – these harmless bits of material about people fancying each other, how big someone's salary is or how a certain decorator burst into tears after staying for the weekend at a certain grandee's house, crying, 'Oh it's so sad! So much money and so little taste!' Gossip, as it has been said, is a moral discussion. In any case, as a doctor's daughter, I am entirely trustworthy with regard to secrets I have sworn not to divulge. Yet in common with most of my close female friends, I find that the joy of secrets is thwarted by our male so-called partners who blab them out at every opportunity.

'I'm sorry,' said my husband the other day after he had leaked the most appalling indiscretion to a dinner party of ten. 'But how am I supposed to remember what's a secret and what's not? It's your fault for not keeping some sort of secrets book and writing down the things I'm not supposed to tell. Anyway no one was surprised.'

Like many of his male friends he considers the leaking of a secret to be par for the course. Secrets don't seem to hold the same value for men as they do for women. And as for when people 'swear' not to tell anyone, I always find the give-away reply is, 'But who would I tell anyway?' Then, you can tell for sure that they are already anticipating the pleasure of passing it on, and just wondering who to tell first.

At least Giles is not as bad as the husband of Nicky, who has learned to her cost not to trust Michael with anything. (He used to blurt out things such as 'What was the result of Jane's pregnancy test?' in front of a room full of people.) Sadly, Nicky can no longer confide in him the marvellous material that comes her way, though she is still able to share it with me. The other day Michael happened to drop by and offered to give me a lift into town. On the way there he said, 'I've got such a good secret, I'm just going to burst. Nicky would divorce me if she knew I'd told you but it's so wonderful that I can't resist.'

He then told me a seriously *schadenfreude*-style secret about a stuck-up acquaintance who had had a humiliating come-uppance. It was a first-rate secret, really prize-winning. 'How did you find out?' I asked, after thanking him profusely for telling me. 'I thought Nicky didn't tell you secrets any more.'

'She doesn't,' he admitted. 'But I'm really cunning. I stand outside the door when she's on the phone and I can usually pick up quite a lot just by listening to what she says.'

For Nicky, of course, to whom knowledge is power, there is little point in amassing all this social data unless one can demonstrate that one 'knew it first'. Sometimes she contents herself with saying 'I already knew that' when the gossip becomes public. At other times, I suspect that she is rather happy to have the sort of husband who can blurt everything out for her and whom she can blame while still retaining her own lily-white reputation.

'Oh sorry, I forgot that was supposed to be secret,' said another girl's boyfriend as she glared at him across the table. 'But once more than one person knows a secret, it's not a secret any more,' he lectured. The secret? The girl's aunt was having an affair, and her mother had confided in her as her first grown-up confidence. She told her boyfriend because she wanted to share the secret with him and he told the room full of people – which happened to include her mother.

One can get secret fatigue. Particularly when there is a run of secrets about married people having affairs. For our little daughter, however, and her contemporaries, the world of secrets remains a dependable source of undiluted joy.

PERMA-FAWLTYISM

'What do you want in your bap? Cheese or Marmite?' asked Giles.

'What are you talking about baps for?' I snarled. 'I thought we had decided on a pub lunch.'

For once on a Sunday the children were in the safe hands of their nanny and we had decided to use the unaccustomed freedom to walk together. We would set off over the downs along an ancient earthwork to a village eight miles distant. There we would quench our thirsts and rest our weary limbs. Yet other anxieties seemed to be opportunistically swarming in to fill up the void created by the children's absence.

'We may well go to a pub,' said Giles. 'But I'm just thinking ahead.' He shook his head like Dixon of Dock Green. 'I can see from here that those running shoes wouldn't support your ankles if you slipped into a rabbit hole. A bap could tide you over until the air ambulance arrived.'

Driving up to the set-off point for our walk we found a pink notice flapping in the breeze. 'Warning – there has been a spate of thefts from this area. Please remove valuables from your parked car.'

'Oh dear,' worried Giles, peering into the Lada, 'perhaps we'd better take the wheel-changing kit with us.'

We decided against it and soon we were striding over the cropped turf under a warming sun. It was a rare pleasure to walk alone together without dawdling children to break the momentum. But it was too good to last. 'Don't you think it's odd that we're the only people on these downs on a glorious June morning?' asked Giles uneasily. Soon, however, he had spotted a solitary speck on the horizon. Another walker was gaining rapidly upon us. We had a choice of either quickening our pace to sustain our lead or stopping to let him overtake us. Above us larks were ascending and clouds were scudding over the majestic chalk downs, yet all we could think about was our rival walker.

'You don't suppose he's some kind of madman? Why is he walking so fast?' said Giles as he watched the figure approach. Soon heavy breathing was audible and the grim-faced athlete panted straight past us, eyes set forward. 'All right?' shouted Giles in a cockney accent to the shrinking figure.

'Well, he looked harmless enough,' I said.

'Yes,' said Giles looking at his watch. 'But what is becoming apparent is that we are miles from any town or village and it's nearly one thirty. It would be awful to miss the pub.' He broke into a panicky run.

'Calm down,' I pleaded. 'It won't matter if we miss the pub. The whole point of today is that it was meant to be worry-free.'

Yet at the foot of the downs we found we had descended to the wrong village despite our careful map-reading. The only pub in the area was three miles away. A four-wheel drive vehicle came grinding along the bridleway behind us.

'Don't smile at him,' seethed Giles. But he was too late. I had already smiled and made an almost involuntary hitch-hiking gesture towards the driver, who slowed to a halt. 'Any chance of a lift to the nearest pub?' grinned Giles, hypocritically.

The stranger nodded silently. He was weird and did look slightly mad, I realised, as we drove along. But how clever I had been to make sure Giles got into the front before I climbed into the back. Otherwise he could have driven off at speed with me, a prisoner.

At the pub Giles sprang out of the car and I tried to. My heart lurched as the vehicle moved off with me child-locked in the back. It was a nasty moment but clearly the driver was not a psychopath. He released me with a short laugh a few yards along the road. As we walked into the pub I breathed a sigh of relief. 'Well, I'm not going to worry about anything else now. I'm just so glad to be alive.'

'Yes, let's just relax and enjoy our lunch now,' said Giles. 'Can we see the menu please, landlord?' he asked in a Wiltshire accent.

'Sorry mate, we don't do lunches.'

IT'S
NOT HIS
FAULT

Tiptoe-ing upstairs the other night at ten o'clock to check that my daughter was asleep, I found her snipping away with some nail scissors. The floor and bed were littered with hundreds of tiny pieces of white paper.

'Freya!' I scolded. 'What on earth are you doing?'

She started in surprise and her lower lip quivered. 'I'm making snow,' she wailed.

'But you're a very naughty girl,' I said. 'Why aren't you asleep?'

'It's not my fault I don't get sleepy at night!' she bawled. 'God made me like this.'

For the first time it was clear to me that, in the matter of whose 'fault' things are, Freya will come down with the Wood way of looking at things. On my side of the family we take the stern Presbyterian view that things are always our own fault. When, for instance, I fell over as a little girl, my parents would say 'Why weren't you looking where you were going?' instead of 'Poor you'. On Giles's side, however, harmony is prized so highly that levelling of blame is virtually unknown.

'Oh dear,' one member of the family might sigh. 'The

shed door was left open and these papers have been rained on.'

'I went in there yesterday so was that my fault?' Giles might ask defensively.

'No, darling, of course not. It was my fault for not checking that you had closed it.'

As the guiltless party returned from his yacht race in time for Sunday lunch last week we cheered 'Hooray! Tell us all about it.'

'Well . . .' Giles hesitated. 'It was quite something to be part of an Armada of yachts racing round the Isle of Wight. We set off from Cowes at eight thirty and eleven hours later we were back where we started and Pip Wood received a pewter tankard.'

'Did you win the race, Daddy?' asked Freya.

'No, Freya. We didn't really expect to. People say it's the taking part that matters most, not whether you win or lose,' he answered in a monotone. 'Would you like me to get out the map and show you where Daddy sailed?'

'Um . . . no thank you,' said Freya, racing out of the room.

'So . . . did you enjoy it?' I asked.

'Well,' he began. 'Towards the end of the race Pip Wood let me get low morale. I was cold and bored and I went down below deck. I suddenly realised how important it was for Churchill to visit the troops on the front line.'

'Surely it wasn't Pip Wood's fault?' I scoffed. 'He would have been concentrating on not colliding with other boats.'

'Oh no, it's up to the captain.' Giles shook his head. 'I went below deck and I started thinking that life was a bit like the round-the-island race. You think you are making progress but you just end up back where you started but feeling exhausted. Pip Wood should have told me we only had an hour to go and boosted my morale.'

'Nothing's ever your fault, is it?' I remarked.

'Not usually,' agreed Giles. 'But unfortunately the stew I made was a disaster and I don't know how it happened.'

The stew he had made for *après*-race consumption had been transported by Tupperware and heated up on the tiny cabin stove whereupon the crew had fallen upon it like carrion crows. And then 'almost choked because it tasted just like Yardley talc'. Despite an inquisition, Giles had found the finger of blame could be pointed at no one but himself. 'We had to chuck it out and eat hot-dogs in a hospitality tent,' he said gloomily.

Suddenly, the mystery was solved. Pip's wife Lois rang to say she had remembered that the previous weekend some concentrated Fairy Liquid had spilt in the cupboard where the pans were stored. So a residual slick of Fairy Excel was to blame for the scented stew. 'So it wasn't your fault after all. Well, that must be a relief!' I laughed.

'Oh I never doubted it for a minute,' said Giles, tucking into his third helping of crackling. 'By the way, Mary, this crackling isn't very crispy.'

'Sorry,' I yawned. 'It must be God's fault for not blessing me with cooking skills.'

BEER

'Did you buy these rotten bananas for any particular reason, Mary?' I had come in through the back door to find Giles lobbing bananas directly from the fruit bowl into the compost bucket.

'Everyone knows that bananas aren't ripe unless they've got that brown speckling!' I cried impotently as the last banana whizzed past me. 'You must be mad. Why throw them out without even opening them?'

Then it dawned on me ... 'Uh-oh. I know what's happened. You've had beer.'

'Of course I've had beer. Every man in Britain will have been drinking beer today,' said Giles. 'This is one of the hottest days since records began.'

'I knew it,' I sighed. 'Beer just makes you so aggressive.'

'Aggressive?' He gave a short laugh. 'What you mean is that I get my spirit back. Normally my true personality is suppressed but beer enables me to be myself and I don't have to live a lie. *In vino veritas.*'

'If only it was vino,' I said. 'It's only beer that makes you like this. Right then,' I said. 'I'm not particularly keen on your true personality so I'll just nip along to the Sandersons' until the effect of the beer wears off.'

While skinheads express their beer-induced aggression through beating up strangers or 'liquid laughs', experience has taught me that my husband prefers more sophisticated acts of veiled aggression such as throwing out food, putting brown 'washes' over paintings that were already finished and spoiling them and worrying at woodworm holes to make them bigger. Recently he even dismantled the plastic paddling-pool while the children were enjoying it. 'We've had the longest day of the year,' he barked. 'That was the twenty-first of June. Now the nights are drawing in and the days are getting shorter.'

I made my escape to the Sandersons' where we discussed the demerits of beer over aggression-defusing champagne and I 'shared' with another woman whose husband turns into Mr Hyde on beer.

'You know you do, darling,' she insisted. 'You do things like deliberately spilling the Bombay Mix into the fleecy rug.'

But by the following morning harmony reigned again as two of our favourite friends were arriving for the weekend, and we were thrilled when Jean-Noël and Lucie announced that they would stay on Sunday night as well. 'Hooray!' we cheered in unison. 'We normally get really bad Sunday Night Syndrome. If you are here we can look forward to it.'

As he prepared their barbecue luncheon on Sunday, Giles suggested he and Jean-Noël crack open some beer. 'By all means,' I said magnanimously. 'I'd welcome the opportunity for some independent witnesses to see your personality change under beer. Especially Lucie, who seems to think you're some kind of saint,' I added pleasantly. But so happy was I that I made the mistake of leaving the barbecue area after lunch as I serially trekked to the kitchen with loads for the dishwasher. Suddenly I realised to my horror that Lucie and Jean-Noël were packing up their Range Rover. 'What's happening?' I panicked.

'Giles has pointed out that it would be irresponsible of us to stay the night here when we have to be in London by ten o'clock tomorrow morning,' said Lucie gloomily.

'What?' I screamed. 'But it is never more than two hours to London, no matter how bad the traffic.'

'You're welcome to stay but I wouldn't take the risk if I were you,' said Giles, pulling a sensible face.

'So sadly . . . I think we'd better be realistic,' said Lucie.

'No, no, no,' I cried, falling to the ground and beating it with my fists. 'It's the beer. Giles doesn't want you to go . . . it's the beer talking.'

But the beer had talked persuasively and my cries fell on deaf ears. Indeed they were even drowned out by the sound of empty cans being crunched in a cruel fist as Lucie and Jean-Noël drove away, leaving me alone with Mr Hyde.

'What a pity they aren't staying,' he said.

'But you made them go!' I shrieked. 'Because of beer again.'

'I know,' Giles sighed. 'The beer has made me so annoying that I've even gone and annoyed myself.'

TEMPORARY
CHIPPINESS

We had been out to lunch nearby and Giles seemed more than usually disturbed.

'Did you say that our host was a self-made man?' he asked.

'Yes,' I replied.

'Did you see the downstairs loo?' he pondered. 'It was lined with hand-printed silk. The pool-house was bigger than our entire cottage and his kitchen garden was the size of our field. Surely he can't have made all that money himself?'

'Why not?' I enquired. 'That's the sort of money you do make in the world of business.'

'He showed me his collection of bonsai vegetables,' continued Giles. 'They were all laid out in neat little rows, much neater than mine. Mind you it's not surprising it looked good, because he can afford help.'

'Yes,' I agreed. 'But then very few men in the prime of life and at the peak of their earning capacity *would* do their own weeding. They see that it doesn't make financial sense when they can pay someone else a hundredth of what they are earning in the world of big business to do the weeding for them. Perhaps you should employ someone else . . .'

'Ah,' said Giles, 'but you miss the point. You can't trust

someone else to weed your garden for you. They'd pull up all the plants.'

'Would that matter?' I spluttered, 'if the alternative was effectively paying a gardener three hundred thousand pounds a year through being unable to go out to work yourself?'

Giles yawned. 'Just occasionally I'd like to meet someone who lives in a Nissen hut,' he snorted.

'Why?' I asked. 'What good would that do you?'

'It wouldn't do me any good,' he answered, 'but Freya is starting to complain that we don't have a pool. When I was her age we got a lot of fun from a hosepipe in the garden. That's all you need,' he said.

Soon he was cursing as he scooped dead insects from our paddling pool with a sieve. 'Daddy, why don't you ever put any money into the swearing box? Are you really that poor?' said Freya.

'No! Not really poor but neither am I rich. We are somewhere in the middle. Not as poor as old Mrs Mudge who collects faggots from the hedgerows in winter, but not as rich as the man we had lunch with who grows miniature vegetables just for the fun of it.'

'But we're growing miniature vegetables too!' she cried. 'Does that mean we are getting richer?'

'Er, no, Freya, that's because it hasn't rained for two months. My word you're a clever little girl, aren't you?'

Just then the telephone went and I had a quick chat with some neighbours in the village. 'That was the Sandersons,' I told Giles. 'They wanted to know if we would like to come up for a swim.'

'UP for a swim? What do they mean up? I know for a fact that the ground slopes away gradually from our cottage to their Georgian rectory because I've seen Freya's tennis ball rolling towards their house of its own accord. Now, had they said "Come across for a swim", "Come along for a swim", even "Come down for a swim", but "Come UP for a swim" . . .'

'Please let's go!' cried Freya and I, and as the temperature was nudging a hundred in our hot little village Giles agreed that we could make our way 'down' to the Sandersons'. In the splashing and the spray that followed it was clear that all petty rivalries and jealousies were instantly forgotten and the thorny question of ownership was wiped out. Particularly as Giles had had a satisfying conversation with Peter Sanderson about the difficulty of running a pool. 'Far more difficult than running a vegetable garden,' he said, 'with endless fuss over chemicals and algae, fishing dead animals out, rolling the cover to and fro, getting the temperature right, then the colour of the water . . .'

'Far better a borrower than a lender be!' winked Giles as we waved goodbye to the Sandersons after our swim and made our way back up through the village to our cottage.

HOME
POLICING

'Right,' said Giles, coming into my little office one Tuesday morning. 'I'm off to work now and I want to make sure you know what your priorities are for the day . . .' Speaking in a loud and hectoring voice he began to list my outstanding chores and to tell me in which order I should tackle them.

'And you've had a request from the health centre that the baby be brought in for a routine hearing test . . .' he barked. 'I suggest you deal with that this afternoon . . .'

'Giles,' I interrupted. 'One. I can decide what my own priorities are. And two. Why don't *you* take the baby in for her hearing test and have one yourself while you're at it. You've obviously gone slightly deaf or you wouldn't need to shout at the top of your voice all the time.'

'I'm far too busy today.'

'Doing what?'

'I don't have to tell you what I'm doing. It's none of your business.'

It couldn't have been a more advantageous moment, as our friend Susie was sitting in my office and witnessing the interchange. When he had gone she said, 'I do worship the ground Giles walks on but I must admit he's difficult.'

A problem shared is a problem halved and as the day went on Susie and I compared notes with so many of our friends with 'control freaks' for husbands that the problem was eventually quartered if not sixthed.

'What I find so exhausting,' said Susie of her husband, 'is that he queries every single thing I do. If I fry an egg he says "You could have used a smaller pan." '

Jo's husband Gerry was top of the tinpots. That morning as she was driving him towards their house in Balham he had said, 'Right here, then left, then . . .'

'Gerry . . .' Jo had interrupted. 'I do this journey four or five times a day and have done so every day for the past seven years.'

'All right then, calm down,' said Gerry. 'I'm only reminding you . . . You know how your mind's not always on the job.'

'Will you take my shoes in to be mended and post my parcel recorded delivery?' Gerry had asked Jo one morning.

'Yes, of course I will,' she had replied pleasantly. A few minutes later, when she was just going out through the front door, Gerry had called her back and, wagging his finger menacingly, had enquired, 'Not so fast. So. What are you going to do while you're out? Come on!'

'I'm going to have your shoes mended and post your parcel recorded delivery,' she gasped in indignation.

'Good,' said Gerry. 'Don't forget.'

Alexa, who doesn't even live with her boyfriend, said that when he came round to her flat, if he had not been there for a day or two he always walked about rearranging a few little things in his own taste before he could sit down and relax.

Having had a deeply satisfying and enjoyable day's gossiping on the telephone I was quite well disposed to Giles when he came back home that evening. I ignored his saying 'I see you've bought a new washing up brush. There was plenty of life in the old one,' and handed him a glass of wine as we sat down in the garden to watch the sunset and do some bonding. I told him the story about Gerry and the parcel. Giles nodded, his face alive with animation as he enjoyed every second of the story.

'So Gerry said, "Good. Just make sure you don't forget," ' I was in the middle of saying.

Giles nodded delightedly. 'And was Jo loving it?' he asked.

'What?' I spluttered. 'What do you mean, was she loving it? Of course not. Why on earth would she love it?'

For a few moments there was a ponderous silence and Giles's facial expression bore testimony to the fact that he was genuinely scouring his unconscious to explain this bizarre interpretation of Jo's reaction. Then he answered. 'When I was a boy I went to the circus with my mother and there were lionesses going around in a ring being made to perform tricks by a man cracking a whip. I remember saying to my mother, "Isn't it very cruel?" And she said, "No. They're loving it".'

FALSE
ECONOMIES

'Stop chopping! You've done at least a month's worth of kindling,' I complained as I looked out of the back door to find my husband continuing to fillet logs into pick-a-stick-sized pieces.

'Well if you're going to insist on buying a car phone, then we'll need to make some economies round here,' said Giles, pushing past me with his load of faggots. 'Oh, and cancel whatever plans you had for this morning. We can't keep ordering logs at forty pounds a load. We're going to have to forage for wood. Come on. Get the children dressed and ready.'

'I can't come now,' I groaned. 'I'm writing a really difficult letter and I've got to finish it.'

My protests fell on deaf ears. In full Basil Fawlty mode Giles moved towards the central heating switch. 'Please don't turn the heating off!' I moaned. 'It's freezing!'

'Everyone knows that if you want to stay warm in a cottage then you've got to keep moving,' Giles lectured. 'It's part of the cottage economy.'

'But I can't keep moving while I'm writing a letter,' I spluttered. Unable and unwilling to imagine the possible savings that might accrue in the long term from having a car phone in the short term, Giles was following in the footsteps of his late father, a career budgeter, who regularly introduced new saving programmes to his family to compensate for extravagances. During the early days of our courtship we often went to Wood Family Headquarters for weekends. There I watched as father and son manhandled tree trunks, foraged from a local hillside, out of the boot of Giles's mother's small hatchback. I noted that his father never used his own car (the 'Flagship') for this purpose.

Sawing and splitting these logs by hand often took up a good part of the day, as did the process of hauling them up the staircase to the first-floor drawing-room. Perhaps a certain amount of money was saved by log-foraging but I calculated that the replacement of my mother-in-law's car, whose suspension was damaged as a result of bearing excessive loads, turned the whole exercise into something of a false economy.

Heating, and saving on heating bills nonetheless continued to preoccupy the Wood family. In the days of ceramic hobs they were not slow to discover the vicissitudes of owning one as, long after turning it off, the ring continued to give off heat while provokingly cooking nothing at all. 'This is dead heat,' Giles's father said, and rigged up two Calor gas camping rings instead.

So conditioned was his son to the idea of saving resources rather than generating new ones that Giles once caused our seven-year-old daughter to experience considerable meta-physical anxiety. He had told her that the sun is a huge ball of fire. 'It's slowly burning itself up,' he said. 'And one day it will burn itself out. So we should make the most of it by getting up early on sunny days to get the free warmth.' Freya was devastated by the idea of an utterly darkened world. 'But it won't affect you,' Giles reasoned. 'You'll have been dead for thousands of years by the time the sun dies.'

Naturally, this made things even worse. But I reassured her. 'There are suns being made all the time. As one burns up nature provides another to take its place.' Is this true? I knew someone who might confirm it for me telephonically but we were in the car. 'We must get a car phone,' I told Giles. 'It will save us from such a lot of stress it will pay for itself in the long run.' To a man who does not change gear if he can help it because 'it uses up more petrol' and who puts on the windscreen wipers only intermittently and by hand, 'to avoid wear and tear', the idea was depressing.

'No, it's not at all "green" to have a mobile telephone. It increases the earth's electromagnetic fields, it may cause brain cancer, it jacks up the whole frantic pace of life and makes people leave things to the last minute that they could easily have done in time had they had no other option. It is just generally morally wrong to own a mobile telephone.'

'But what if I told you that my mother had offered to buy one for me and pay for the calls on it?'

'Oh, well in that case, if your mother's going to pay for it, that's completely different! That's wonderful news. How soon can we get one?'

As it happened, my mother was not planning to pay for my mobile telephone. I had put it to Giles hypothetically and he misunderstood me. Nevertheless it struck me that variations of this device could be used in the future to get to the bottom of how a husband really feels about a potential purchase.

The great-aunt of a friend of mine had a blissfully happy marriage for forty years. Her nephew told me that the secret of the marriage's success was that, having realised early on that her husband was fanatically keen on saving money, she, though naturally extravagant, became interested in saving it herself, rather than battling through the rest of their lives together in a state of constant opposition.

'They always had the cheapest possible things, never entertained, cooked on gas rings, always used second-class stamps,' said Jonny. 'Then, towards the end of her life my aunt became really quite angry. She was lying in bed with pneumonia, which she recovered from, when she overheard her husband making enquiries about the cheapest possible coffins available. She never quite forgave him for that . . .'

MONDAY
MORNING
MALAISE

Like Seasonal Affective Disorder, Monday Morning Malaise
has joined the list of medically accredited syndromes. The
fact that huge numbers of people have to be roused from
their beds as though from comas and that they have the
sensation of paddling in a pool of treacle until around lunch-
time on a Monday, is now recognised as a physical condition.

It is a variation of jet lag, and caused by the natural
tendency to sleep in on Saturday and Sunday mornings, thus
throwing the body-clock out of kilter in time for Monday.

Knowing that things are officially more difficult than usual,
however, doesn't make Monday mornings any easier, and
the malaise is bound to be exacerbated in a household where
a small child has to be got ready for school and sent out of the
house with a variable list of requisites. In our daughter's case
a typical list might include:

An orange and a carton of cloves (to make a
pomander);
A signed legal indemnification form (now necessary
each time the children go on a school trip to outwit
the new breed of suing-opportunity parents);

Ballet kit;
Gym kit;
Cheque for ballet exam;
Cheque for school uniform shop.

To say nothing of reading book, spelling book, pencil case and contents, lip salve, hanky and hairband.

Although only one and a half hours had elapsed since we woke up, by the time Giles's car finally trundled off to school, I was already exhausted as I stood amidst the chaos. What joy when Melly, our nanny, arrived and I could reel into my office for a few moments of peace.

But at five past nine there was already the sound of heavy breathing from outside the door, and an annoying hand rattling at the handle.

'What do you want, Giles?' I groaned.

'I'd like to clear up a few points.'

'Please, I beg you, leave me alone. I must seize these precious moments of mental clarity to plan my work schedule before things get on top of me.' The rattling went on insidiously until I unlocked the door in fury. 'All right, what is it now?' I snapped. 'Have you lost your glasses again? Or are you going to wait at the garage all day while your car is being serviced, because you have forgotten to arrange a courtesy car?'

'There's no need to be unpleasant. I just want to talk to you about our day.'

'Well talk then – there's no need to shout. Have you had your ears tested?'

'Now, we've got a lot to discuss,' said Giles, settling down happily in anticipation.

'This isn't a good time to discuss a lot of things.'

'When is a good time? We had guests all weekend. In the evenings we don't put the children to bed till eight thirty, then you fall fast asleep after one glass of wine . . .'

The phone rang, interrupting us.

'I can't talk now, Susie,' I said. 'I'll ring you back. I'm feeling a bit irritable.' Looking round, however, I saw Giles had disappeared. 'Where are you?' I called.

'Here!' he called back from the kitchen. 'Just making some coffee.'

'What's the hold up?' I shouted, a few minutes later.

'Just waiting to push the filter down.'

He came back into the office and settled into a chair. 'Right, as I said, we have a lot to discuss.'

'Get on with it then.'

'Point number one – holidays. We can't get through the winter without one.'

'Holidays!' I screamed. 'We need to discuss work.'

'Point number two,' he overruled me. 'Loo paper.'

'What about loo paper?'

'We've run out.'

'Well what is there to discuss? Do you think Michael Heseltine discusses the fact that they've run out of loo paper with his wife in the mornings?'

'Point number three – Christmas. Who is seeing whom, where and when?'

'Please, Giles,' I begged, as the thought of Christmas made my head begin to spin. If our previous problems were like paddling in a pool of treacle, Christmas is like trying to swim in one, as we try to juggle five sets of relations in five different locations of the British Isles. 'Leave me alone, Giles, please.'

'Unless you learn to tackle these problems, you'll never learn to resolve them,' he said, wagging his finger. 'And point number four . . . this cheque has just arrived in the post.'

'Oh, what wonderful news, darling!' I cheered.

Money certainly talks. My mood was quite different. 'Can I have a hug now?' he asked.

'A compromise hug,' I said, still feeling a bit irritable, and allowed him to hug me backwards rather than frontwards.

ARGUING
IN
PUBLIC

My mother would never have dreamed of quarrelling with my father in public. I can hardly remember her even quarrelling with him at home in front of her children. Things are different for a modern couple.

It is not so much that one seeks out the chance to parade before a wider audience the niggling arguments that typify married life. It is more that the pace of our life became so relentless with the arrival of our second child, that it is a fact that if grievances are not aired as they happen, then they will never be aired at all, since there will simply not be time to go into a dignified sulk and bring them up later in the privacy of the home. By then there will be something else on the agenda.

The occasions when the public most regularly enter our lives as a sort of Greek chorus are shopping trips on which Giles must accompany me. Often it is Waitrose which turns out to be the forum for a public dispute. At the fish counter one Friday, for example:

'Oh, let's have plaice tonight,' said Giles.

'No, I can't stand its lack of texture. Let's have mackerel with pesto mash.'

'Mackerel? I always think mackerel's the sort of fish that only pelicans eat.' He looked to the fishmonger for support. It was not forthcoming.

'Have you decided, madam?' asked the fishmonger politely, while a queue twitched behind us, with eyes rolling and shoulders shrugging.

'Sorry to be so indecisive,' I apologised to the stony-faced queue before settling on herrings as a compromise.

'Please don't spend too long in here,' Giles begged me. So I made my way briskly down an aisle and flung a packet of frozen peas into the trolley.

'Oh, no you don't,' called Giles, as he lobbed the packet straight back into the freezer. 'Has it ever occurred to you that Waitrose's own brand of pea might be cheaper and exactly the same quality? Look!' he shouted, waggling a bag of peas so close to my face that I could not focus on the price. 'Which brings me to my next question – have you ever looked at the price of anything before you buy it? Or have you simply not made the connection between our overdraft and your extravagance?'

A number of other shoppers were hovering near us, exchanging knowing glances. 'Has it ever occurred to you to make the connection between shopping here and working here?' I asked. 'Or have you not made the connection between working and money? – because I see they pay two hundred and sixty pounds a week for people to load the shelves.'

Now we were at the check-out. 'I saw you had bought a one-hundred-watt bulb so I changed it for a sixty,' he said.

'Why? I wanted a one-hundred-watt bulb.'

The friendly assistant looked up. 'Oh, I'm afraid I've put that sixty-watt bulb through.'

'It's all right,' I said. 'But just don't interfere, Giles.'

'If I didn't interfere, you'd be up the creek without a paddle,' chortled Giles, nodding complicity at the cashier.

'How come you always choose this check-out lady?' I whispered. 'She has seen us arguing at least three times before.'

'Because I've heard her saying, "It takes all sorts". I think she really enjoys our arguments.'

'Well, I don't enjoy her listening to them,' I scowled.

'Then you must learn not to answer back,' said Giles.

'What?' I almost screamed.

'Don't worry,' said Giles, with a mollifying caress, 'I only do it to cheer her up. I've heard her saying it makes her week when we come in.'

WEEKEND
IN A
STATELY
HOME

Some months after Kate visited our cottage with her new suitor, the stately home owner, they invited us to stay with them for a weekend.

'At least we'll have some good food and fine wine,' said Giles. 'What a pity you had to buy leather off-cuts when they came to us. Normally my pigeon casserole is a triumph.'

'It wouldn't have mattered whether it was a triumph or not,' I answered, 'given that aristocrats think pigeon is vermin.'

'An Englishman's home is his castle,' said Giles irrelevantly, and I could tell from the look on his face that a weekend of point-scoring lay ahead.

After a four-hour drive the Lada finally trundled round a hairpin bend to reveal the sprawling stately in its parkland, and we pulled up outside the imposing oak entrance doors. Yet, as I made my way inside, I noticed that Giles was not with me. I found him outside, picking up some flaking paint on a window frame.

'What a nightmare!' he enthused. 'If he doesn't catch this soon he'll have to replace the whole window. Just multiply that by four hundred and you'll see why I'm very happy to live in a cottage!'

Soon we were being shown into a heavenly set of rooms but once we were alone I saw Giles's mouth had contracted to the size of a button. 'Why are we on the ground floor?' he objected. 'As an artist I would have preferred an elevated prospect from my window.'

'Stop complaining,' I sighed as I wandered happily about the giant rooms, displaying my things on the many empty surfaces and hanging our clothes in a mahogany wardrobe the size of our own bedroom at home.

'I suppose earls don't care tuppence that an electric fire is the most uneconomic way to heat a room,' came Giles's next gripe. 'I wonder if he's ever heard of Economy 7. Look, there's a Dimplex heater full on. It's probably been on all day. His heating bills must be astronomical. It's not even cold outside . . .'

Like a human bluebottle he was interrupting my reverie and fantasy of self-importance. 'Oh stop it,' I said. 'You've got enough problems of your own without worrying about his heating bills. Why don't you try and enjoy being here before Labour gets in?'

Blissful silence reigned for a few moments but then a muffled knocking from the bathroom alerted me to the fact that Giles was now conducting an unsolicited structural survey. 'And what's this damp patch on the bathroom wall? You'd think with all those Rembrandts and Van Dycks that he could afford to slap on a bit of Aquaseal,' he tutted.

'Interesting, isn't it?' I snapped. 'You yourself have a cottage which would fit into this set of rooms, yet you haven't got round to dealing with your own damp patch. At least it shows you've got more in common with him than you thought.'

'Quite,' said Giles. 'We've both got damp patches! Chop,

chop,' he bossed. 'We're due in the Round Room for drinks.'

Soon we were striding through the dimly-lit rooms of the treasure house. 'I think it's a bit of an affectation to have the lights down this low,' said Giles.

Our host was sitting by a huge log fire. 'Champagne?' He indicated a bottle on a nearby table. Giles's mouth closed up again. 'I'm afraid champagne doesn't agree with me at the moment. I think I'd like to start with a Coke.'

'Help yourself,' said Lord X.

'But . . .' Giles paused for full effect. 'There doesn't seem to be any ice.'

'That's because there isn't any. Ice has been a rare commodity in this house ever since the ice house in the garden fell into disrepair.'

The room, we now noticed, was lit entirely by candle-light. 'There's been a power cut, so I've ordered a take away from the local Indian restaurant,' said our host.

'An Indian take away!' the other guests cheered. 'What fun!'

Some Margaux 1982 stood enticingly on the table. 'And wouldn't it be even more authentic to have lager or beer instead of wine with the curry?' suggested one unhelpful guest.

'Good idea,' said the earl.

'This isn't the life,' hissed Giles in my ear.

'Make yourself at home,' said Lord X, handing Giles a box of poppadams.

Giles was exultant. 'Sorry?' he said. 'Oh, I must have been daydreaming; I thought I *was* at home.'

SMALL
SATISFYING
JOBS

'May I suggest you don't scrunch up your waste paper,' said Giles, grappling around my desk. 'If you drop paper straight into a bin, it takes up less surface area so the bin doesn't have to be emptied once an hour.'

'But there's no satisfaction in dropping paper into a bin carefully!' I cried. 'The whole point of scrunching it up is to show that you've dealt with that bit of paper. It's a deliberate act of aggression. Anyway, why are you interfering in my office?'

'Because, unlike you, I'm getting on with my day,' he barked.

When either of us starts emptying waste-paper baskets, it is a sure sign that we are doing just the opposite of getting on with our day. We are putting off more urgent business by performing Small Satisfying Jobs to give the illusion of progress.

Later I found Giles in the bathroom padlocking one half of a pair of scissors to the towel rail. 'We waste so much time each week looking for these nail scissors. Now we'll never lose them again.'

'But we'll never use them either!' I raged. 'It's too difficult to manipulate them from that angle. Where's the key?'

'I've hidden it,' he said, staring at me with a tinpot dictator's expression on his face.

Our argument was interrupted by the arrival of the postman. One of my own Small Satisfying Projects had come to fruition with the arrival of mail-order sun-visors.

'Wait till you see these,' I told Giles, who stood impatiently by as the Terminator-style wrap-around visors emerged from their packaging. 'There you are,' I said, handing them to him. 'They're to be worn over existing glasses. They'll help to arrest that terrible quilting you've started to get around your eyes from screwing them up in sunlight.'

HOW TO PUT WASTE PAPER INTO A BIN:

RIGHT   WRONG

'How much were they?' he asked ungratefully, as he tried them on over his tortoiseshells. They fell to the floor with a clatter of cheap plastic. 'Typical,' he said. 'They're far too big for any normal human to wear.'

'It's not their fault your nose is too perpendicular!' I countered.

'Anyway, why are you wasting time arguing, when we've got so much more important stuff on our agendas?' we accused each other simultaneously. Actually we were both trying to delay thinking about the massive organisational nightmare of our daughter's forthcoming seventh birthday party.

'Let's tackle that now,' said Giles. 'You've obviously left it too late to get an entertainer and this year I don't want you wasting a fortune on party bags. Each child can have a sugar cube instead of sweets. They all prefer them.'

The day continued in this manner until about five o'clock when Giles entered my office to announce 'The day's virtually gone. As we're making no progress, let's do a big shop.' Shopping at least gives a bogus sense of achievement, so we made our way to Waitrose.

The total tally for our two trolley-loads was horrific but we were distracted by a man whom we had met twice at dinner. He was at the next check-out and his cards were being rejected. 'I'm going to ask you a big favour,' he drawled.

Giles's mouth pursed but I rushed forward to pay £80.74.

'Thanks, you're a star,' drawled our friend of a friend as he swanned out of the store.

'That's a bit casual,' said Giles. 'Does he even know where we live? And look, quick, his wife's in tears in the car. They've obviously lost all their money in Lloyds and we'll never get ours back.'

As it happened this very nice friend of a friend turned up at our cottage the very next morning with the £80.74. 'You saved my life,' he said. 'My wife was in the most terrible state already because we'd just taken our boy to boarding-school for his first term. She was in floods. It would really have been the last straw if we couldn't have got that stuff from Waitrose.'

So that was the reason she was crying – the night of mild anxiety we had suffered had been quite unnecessary. Nevertheless we were grateful to the couple. The worry about possibly losing £80.74 had been a Small Satisfying Worry and just enough to quite take our minds off the far more taxing problem of planning the party.

TIREDNESS

'How come you're being so nice this morning?' asked Giles.

'It's because you're being less annoying than usual,' I answered amiably. Secretly I knew the real reason – though I was not amiable enough to admit it. For once I had had enough sleep.

The trouble with not having enough is that you tend to forget that this is the reason why you are crabbed, why each day seems to be jinxed, and why the person you live with is one of the most cruel and maddening alive. When our baby was about sixteen months she would wake six or seven times a night and have to be rocked or jiggled back to sleep each time. Climbing on to the bed at night, I felt like a member of the fire brigade. Ahead lay a seven-hour shift, not of restorative stupor but of a fitful half-sleep as I waited on red alert to be summoned by bawls. Giles, bless him, slept through the night as though under anaesthetic. He was not unwilling to help – indeed he spent every night between seven pm and ten thirty jumping up and down like a jack-in-the-box in order to reassure and rock little Posy back to the Land of Nod. Friends advised that the traditional solution is that father and mother take it in turns to be on night duty but by the time Giles was roused from his coma the baby would be inconsolable and I would be wide awake myself. Still, at least he made a show of solidarity by saying 'I didn't sleep at all well' when he came round in the mornings.

We crabbed can live with our own crabbidity. The sense of martyrdom and self-pity can be rewarding in its own way. Yet, 'Tiredness is the mother's greatest enemy,' intones Betty Parsons, the birth and life guru who sees all sorts of marital difficulties arising out of nothing more than sleep deprivation irritability. But it's surprising how one can become used to suffering, almost rather attached to it. Then it takes a short sharp shock to break the cycle.

This happened one morning when Giles returned from the Round the Island race in which he had served as crew on Pip Wood's boat.

'Cancel everything,' he said, arriving ashen-faced at the front door. 'I didn't get a wink of sleep on Pip Wood's boat.'

'What is a wink of sleep, Daddy?' asked Freya.

'What happened to Daddy,' said Giles, 'is that he didn't just have a bad night's sleep, he had no night's sleep at all.'

'So what?' I shrugged. 'Join the club.'

'You don't understand,' said Giles. 'I may overheat or start hallucinating or something. And you know that insomnia is a vicious circle. It could mean that I never sleep again.'

'Good,' I cheered. 'You could do with some extra time to get on with your work.'

'Oh, let me talk to my mother about it. She'll know what to do,' he said, barging past me towards the telephone.

A few minutes later I heard him spelling out the details in grave tones. 'Well, I went to bed at midnight having very stupidly eaten a cheeseburger at about eleven,' he began. 'First I heard the clock strike one. [Pause.] Then I heard it strike two [pause], then three, then four . . .'

'Surely she's got the message by now . . .' I cut in.

'Don't interrupt me, Mary, this is important . . .' Then

five, then I didn't hear six strike so I must have been half asleep for an hour . . . only to be woken up at seven for a gruelling day's sail-training for the Round the Island race.'

His mother's advice was characteristically sound and sensible. 'Ah,' Giles nodded solemnly. 'So you think that in the normal course of events nature will help me to catch up on the lost night of sleep? Well I'm glad someone's interested in my health because Mary certainly doesn't seem to be.'

With the baby, I was in no mood to be interested in an adult's sleep problem. Yet perhaps it was this last straw which provided me with the impetus I needed as I finally forced myself to read *Solve Your Child's Sleep Problem* by Dr Richard Ferber. The book had been given to us months before by a friend who assured us that the techniques described therein would work. The trouble was, we were always too tired to read it.

Finally I put the advice into practice. Giles found me standing at the bottom of the stairs, an oven timer ticking, while the baby bawled her head off in the bedroom.

'Basically, you let the baby cry for five minutes,' I explained: 'Then you go in with a firm expression on your face, see that she is all right and tuck her down again. No cuddling or milk. Then you leave a gap of ten minutes before going in again, then fifteen, so she gets the message that she hasn't been abandoned but she'll be bored with the amount of crying she has to do before you come.'

The author had suggested that the first few nights might not be easy but that the method would work in the end. We were just arguing about whether our particular baby was too stubborn to be manipulated like this when the crying stopped and a happy yawn came over the baby alarm before silence descended.

It worked on the first night and has continued to work. As Dr Ferber explained, all those hours Giles had spent jiggling the cot and pulling the musical cottage were in fact preventing little Posy-Albertine from falling asleep on her own. The ability to do this is innate and present in all children at birth but then their parents drum it out of them by teaching them to need cues.

'That's very good,' congratulated our friend Cyril when I gave him the happy news. 'Perhaps you could use the same method with Giles?'

'What do you mean?' I asked.

'Well, in future, whenever he starts talking about his health, put your earplugs in, set the oven timer for five minutes, then take out the earplugs. If he's still talking about his health, reset the oven timer for ten, then for fifteen . . .'

PHOTO
ALBUMS

When I was a child I used to creep into my parents' bedroom. Once inside I would cringingly creak open the drawer of the linen cupboard where all our family photographs were kept. I had to be surreptitious because I was known to have a propensity for wreaking havoc in the photo drawer.

With the typical child's ability to think only in the short term it used to seem inordinately important to me that I cut out the heads of certain key people from the photographs so that I could put them into lockets. School photographs were particularly vulnerable to this practice and now I despair when I look at the colander-like scrolls. The sight of a school photograph always brings back so vividly that pregnant moment when the whole school concentrated as one on not moving and for once we heard the wind in the trees.

The key difference between my own photograph collection now and the one still held by my mother is that while hers still fits into the same drawer, mine takes up a chest of them. Her collection, the most part of which is black and white, is also so much more chic and meaningful than mine. Less really is more when it comes to photographs.

But though Giles and I have stopped being quite so button happy we still generate at least one bulging packet of thirty-six photographs per month. He is desperate to edit them as we go along, chucking out all but the very best but, neurotically, I want to keep every one of them, 'Just in case . . .,' I say.

'Just in case what?' he queries.

'Well, just in case, for instance Emma loses all her photographs in a fire, then we would be able to give her some of ours that we don't particularly want . . .' I say lamely.

'I can't stand it!' shouts Giles in frustration. 'We have so many photographs now it's actually turning into a threat situation.'

We all know that the recipe for happiness includes not accumulating material goods, but do photographs count as material goods? Are they not more akin to spiritual goods?

Yet for the button-happy there is also the danger of losing the capacity to enjoy real moments and real landscapes because they are too busy taking the photographs. Before books could be bought it is said that the average Ancient Greek could attend a play and afterwards remember every line of the script. No one could do that now because we all know we can have a script if we want to refer to it again. Are we not equally losing the capacity to concentrate on real life with omnipresent cameras and videos?

A friend of mine who is something of a superwoman is such a high achiever that not only does she hold down full-time jobs, write books and manage a family of five children, she has also collected for each of her five children photographs with particular relevance to them and prepared five separate albums. Each photograph in the album is extensively captioned.

'What a shame . . .' I said to Charlie, a family friend, the last time I was in Ireland and legally rifling through the photo drawers. 'No one knows who this is.'

He looked at the photo disparagingly. 'I have no interest in my ancestors,' he said. 'But if you could tell me what was going to be happening next year I'd be interested . . .'

Even as I write, photographic and video mountains are being generated all over the land. I think how lucky I am that my mother has only the one, manageable drawer of photographs. If we died tomorrow we would be loading our daughters with the most horrifying amounts of unidentifiable photographs and making them inevitably feel terribly guilty about those they throw out. How do you throw out an absolutely sweet photograph of people you have never met?

'One thing about photo albums,' said a mother at the school. 'They're a very good reason not to get divorced.'

CAFFEINE
POISONING

'Stop pulling that face!' shouted Freya.

'What face?' asked Giles.

'Don't move and I'll show you with a mirror,' said Freya.

'Oh,' said Giles, 'I see what you mean.'

This familiar facial expression where the features appear to have been pulled upwards by invisible strings resembles that of a victim of a mild case of strychnine poisoning. It is an outward symbol of inner confusion. 'It's the weather!' said Giles. 'I can't decide what to wear this morning. From inside it looks like a glorious summer's day so I put on a T-shirt. As I step outside a black cloud appears and I feel like a resident of Spitzbergen. I then put on my jersey, the sun comes out and it's like Athens airport. I'm taking it personally.'

'Calm down and stop talking rubbish,' I scolded.

'I feel like the poor roses. Just as they were tricked into new growth by last week's heatwave, late frosts have cut them down again. Tell me the point of that. It all suggests a fundamental lack of order or guiding principle in nature.'

'How many cups of coffee have you had?' I asked wearily.

'Three.'

'That explains it. You've got caffeine poisoning again.

Why don't I make you up a mixture of cocculus in water to calm you down?' I urged.

Giles ignored this offer. 'Are you coming to see Pip Wood's boat or not? Yes or no? No!'

The telephone interrupted my answer. It was Lucie, telling us that Normandy was off for half-term.

'Great,' breathed Giles. 'That's one less decision to make. That only leaves nine hundred and ninety-nine other possible destinations to choose from.'

Freya's half-term is prime quality time. It provides the only opportunity in May to make it worthwhile for the whole family to go abroad for a few days, or even to go to members of our own family or friends in remote parts of the British Isles.

'But Jo wants to know if we could go to Yorkshire instead that week and we couldn't decide.'

'It's only May,' groaned Giles, 'and already the summer is getting booked up. Then the summer holidays are lurking on the horizon, guaranteed to bring on another dose of decision fatigue.'

Hoping the weather might help us rule out driving to the south coast, we looked in dismay at the sunshine. The coffee toxins were still surging around his system. Giles swore it would be nose-to-tail all the way and I couldn't decide whether to bring the baby or not.

'Well it's ten o'clock now and Pip said it's not worth our while going if we don't arrive before eleven,' snapped Giles. 'So it won't be worth going if we don't get off right now this minute.'

Inevitably the Lada joined a snail trail of other coast-bound traffic set to enjoy the short Arctic summer.

'We're not going to make it,' said Giles, overtaking BMWs and mounting the pavement in a bid to ignore the snarl-ups.

Soon we were trapped in the one-way system at Lymington, circling too fast to spot the signs to the elusive 'yacht haven' and with a driver unwilling to stop to ask anyone's advice. Finally we saw little Pip Wood walking jauntily along the road and smiling pleasantly. 'So glad you made the decision to come!'

No one will ever know whether it was the right decision to take a one-year-old out on Pip's maiden voyage in his new boat. But as we chugged out towards the Isle of Wight there was no doubt that Pip had made the right decision to buy the boat in the first place. Sheltering below deck, I was blissfully unaware that Giles and Lois were struggling to raise the huge mainsail in a heaving sea complete with inky black sky.

'The wind's really got up,' said Pip, looking puzzled. 'I think we'll head back for port. Take that sail down.'

'I think that was definitely the right decision,' said our skipper without a moment's hesitation.

'Definitely,' said Giles. 'Actually we might easily have been in serious trouble if we hadn't come in. If only all decisions were matters of life and death,' he sighed. 'They would be so much easier to make.'

PMT
TIME

'I really feel that Giles is one of the most sadistic creeps who has ever lived. Now that I look back on our life together I see quite clearly that he has done nothing except slowly and systematically try to do all within his power to make my life a complete and utter misery . . .'

'Just hang on a minute, my dear,' interrupted our sixty-one-year-old friend Jonny, to whom I had been droning on. Jonny is a writer specialising in emotional and medical matters. 'I'm quite sure that Giles is the most charming and thoroughly nice person,' he insisted. 'Could you by any chance be suffering from PMT?'

'Well I do have PMT but that's not the reason . . .' I choked self-pityingly.

Secretly, at the back of my mind, I knew it was the reason. At PMT time, however, one is loath to admit that all the terrible misery might simply be a result of plunging or surging hormones. One wants to blame someone and the most obvious repository of blame is that sadistic creep who has done everything within his power . . . etcetera.

One friend, Susie, refers to her condition as PMV – premenstrual violence. She described a typical example of

PMV the other day. 'I was fast-forwarding a video and when I got to the place where I wanted it to stop I pressed the stop button but it didn't work and the video went whizzing on. Mal [her husband] said "Hey! Press the stop button!" and I just hurled the controls at him. I burst into tears and said "When are you going to stop trying to undermine my self-confidence? It's just so destructive of you and so draining on me!" '

Despite having every sympathy with fellow PMT sufferers I have to admit that the displays of pointless hysteria the condition provokes are faintly embarrassing to witness.

I was at a point-to-point with Stella and Roland and their three daughters. Stella went off to place a bet. Roland, left in charge of three under-sixes, smiled as he tried to restrain them from throwing themselves under the hooves of the horses. 'Stella always wanders off at point-to-points and we can't find her for hours,' he commented pleasantly.

Some time later, after swimming through the sea of faces until almost hypnotised, we found Stella again. 'I told Mary you always wandered off at point-to-points,' said Roland amiably.

Stella's face darkened in fury. 'Ah do not,' she growled in her Glaswegian accent. 'Ah have never once in my whole life wandered off at a point-to-point. You must be going mad. You must literally have gone mad to have said that.'

'Oh gosh, you've got PMT, haven't you?' said Roland. 'Uh-oh. Okay, forget I spoke.'

'Ah certainly will not. It has nothing to do with PMT. How dare you accuse me of always wandering off? Right, that's the last time Ah go anywhere with you.'

'Just cool it, Stella. Just accept that you've got PMT.'

'If you mention PMT again, Ah'm going home without you. Ah've got the car keys you know!'

One day I saw Giles wielding some scissors – but not for his usual maddening motive which is to use them as secateurs and then leave them in the garden to rust. He was cutting out a story from the court proceedings section of the paper. 'Man Lived in Fear of PMT Wife' was the headline. Giles was going to post it to a friend who lives abroad and whose wife literally does jump out from behind doors and club him on the head shouting 'Push your hair back!' or 'That'll teach you to put the butter into the fridge so it's too hard to eat!'

We both chuckled but, in the end, we decided not to send the cutting. What if she opened the letter or saw it while she had PMT? Why, it might put his life at risk.

BRAVERY
IN OUR
TIME

'Phew! I am exhausted,' said Giles, collapsing into a hammock. 'And I am going to put my feet up for the first time this year.'

'That's fine,' I said, 'but what exactly are you exhausted from? Just remind me – this morning you've pottered at your hobby, gardening, then you cooked Sunday lunch and ate it . . .'

'The tragedy is that I've eaten too much crackling,' said Giles, holding his stomach as if wounded.

'Poor Daddy,' said Freya.

'Oh really!' I tutted. 'You've eaten too much crackling. What would you have done if you'd been in the War? It wouldn't have been much good saying you couldn't fight because you had indigestion.'

'All I know is that I can't do anything until someone's brought me a cup of peppermint tea and a Bendick's Bittermint. That might settle my stomach,' he said.

'I wonder how you two would have managed in the trenches?' I said to our friend Cyril, who was lying in an adjacent hammock, his head in the newspapers. Cyril and his family had joined us for the VE Day fiftieth anniversary weekend. He looked up vaguely.

'What?'

'I said what you two need is a spell in the trenches.'

'Weren't the trenches in the First World War?' he countered. 'Anyway, one of the reasons why soldiers fought in the Second World War was to safeguard the freedom of Englishmen to lie in their hammocks after lunch. I am sure we would be very brave in a war. We just haven't had the opportunity.'

Giles put his thumb up and helped himself to a Bittermint fetched by his devoted daughter.

The following afternoon we drove to Aldbourne to celebrate VE Day. There was a brass band, a march by veterans and a delicious outdoor tea made by the Women's Institute and served free to all who came to the village green. The procession of old soldiers marched by to the respectful applause of those lining the green. The assembled children were silent, their little faces momentous. They could sense there was something special about these men and women.

'I feel so ashamed to be a member of our generation,' I said to Cyril's wife, Ursula, dabbing my eyes. 'Just think of the bravery of laying down their lives for what they believed in and then the Beatles came along and spawned a whole generation of divorcing petty criminals.'

All the adults in our group were emotionally drained by the experience, but glad we could show the children living history. Far from being frightened by the tale of the War, they clearly found it inspiring and stood solemnly for the two minutes' silence later that night. 'I did think about the dead soldiers,' said Freya afterwards.

But a moment later, as we were watching a bonfire on a nearby hill, Ursula came into the garden, looking distressed.

'I'm afraid the loo's all bubbling up like a witch's cauldron,' she sighed.

'Oh dear,' I said. 'The cesspit probably needs to have rods or pipes put down it or something disgusting. Giles, there's an emergency, please will you come and deal with it?'

'Why don't you call the man?' came his voice from the hammock.

'You are that man. Here's your opportunity to be brave!' I shouted.

'But one of the great social revolutions of the past fifty years is the chance for women to have equal opportunities. Why don't you deal with it?'

'Because I am not strong enough to lift the manhole cover off,' I said. 'Nor is my stomach strong enough to look at what's underneath.'

'So men have their uses after all!' said Giles, prising off the lid and dealing with the offending foreign object in a true display of peace-time bravery.

A true display of peacetime bravery.

PROJECTION

In early autumn the swallows begin to gather on the telephone wires in our village, but an even surer sign of the turning of the year is the appearance at my office window of Giles with a piece of sandpaper.

'What's happening?' I groan, when the seasonal rasping begins. 'You did the windows last year.'

'Yes,' says Giles, his face drawn back in a rictus of concentration. 'And the year before that. And the marvellous thing is that the weather conditions are exactly right for me to do the job over these next few days, so I'll really be able to get on with it.'

The process of sanding down the frames, scraping out the rotten wood, filling it with linseed putty to recreate the window frame, allowing this to dry, then painting, seems to take an unwarrantably long time.

'I don't see why you can't get some sort of bob-a-job boy to do the bodging and filling instead of you doing it yourself,' I whined this year.

'Because don't you remember what Harry said about me?' Giles grinned. Harry, his best friend/worst enemy from school, now living in Kenya, still manages to unnerve Giles each time he pays a short visit to England. Last time he came over the commented on Giles's liking for Small Satisfying Jobs. 'Giles is the only person I know who's gone from being a bob-a-job boy in his schooldays to being a bob-a-job man in adult life,' said Harry. 'I'm a bob-a-job man!' sang Giles, tauntingly.

I fled from my office to get away from the rasping, to which he had now added a workman's whistle. I made my escape to the bathroom, where I telephoned my friend Jo. As we exchanged updates on the latest atrocities perpetrated by husbands, we also compared the sizes of the mountains of paperwork we would finally be able to get around to tackling now the children were back at school after the summer holidays. Suddenly there was a clunk of a ladder against the window and a boiler-suited figure appeared.

'If you've got a mountain of paperwork to get through, then I suggest you get on with it now,' Giles tutted. 'There's really no excuse for you to be using precious time and money making non-essential calls to Jo if you're as busy as you say you are. Is this what you normally do with your day? No wonder you're always behind with your work.'

'I can't possibly work with you making scraping and rasping noises at my office window!' I retorted.

'I've finished sanding your office window so you can go back in there now,' he smiled.

The nightmare continued throughout the day. Each time I settled into a room it seemed that Big Brother would appear at the window to spy on me. Even when I was in my own office taking telephone calls, he would appear outside making winding signals and mouthing 'wind it up now!' Finally I stormed into the garden. 'Right! I'm ringing the Mayday employment agency to get a proper workman out to finish these windows.'

'Why?' asked Giles. 'It's quite normal for a man to want to protect his nest. All over Britain, men are casting a weather eye over their properties, battening down the hatches and tidying things up in preparation for the ravages of winter. You mustn't strip me of this primeval right.'

'How many more days?'

'Three. And one of them I'll be spending watching the paint dry,' he teased.

'Right, then I'm going to London for the next three days.'

I rang up Ann, our much older friend who has a house in Kensington where we sometimes stay when we are in London and where I used to live when I was first going out with Giles in the early Eighties. 'Can I come and stay for a few days?' I asked. 'Giles is doing the windows again and the annoyance level is just intolerable.'

Ann is not only older than us, but wiser. 'Poor you!' she mocked. 'Is Giles stopping you from getting on with reading magazines and ringing your friends up for a chat? I know all about this. My contemporaries are all married to men of retiring age, and they are hating their husbands finding out how little they do with their days. Rosamund in particular – her husband left the house at seven-fifteen every morning for thirty-five years. Now he's hanging around the house seven days a week, and he keeps asking her, "What on earth have you been doing with your time all these years?"'

'What do you mean?' I asked irritably.

'Well, it must be very difficult for you to cover up that you're just quietly and happily wasting time, if Giles is working at the window of the room you're supposed to be working in.

'Haven't you heard of transference or projection?' Ann continued to tease. 'All married couples are guilty of it. You get annoyed with the person you're married to because they act as your conscience. You're really annoyed with yourself!'

It's a fair cop.